# THE SHORT SALE — PROJECT WORKBOOK

Short Sale Control System (SSCS)

James R. Calder

Shepherd Works Press

# COPYRIGHT



This publication is provided for informational, structural, and organizational purposes only. It does not constitute legal, financial, accounting, tax, or investment advice. Users are encouraged to consult qualified professionals regarding specific transactions.

Neither the author nor the publisher assumes responsibility for any loss, claim, or liability arising directly or indirectly from the use of this workbook.

**SINGLE-TRANSACTION LICENSE NOTICE**



First Edition

ISBN: 978-1-972137-99-4

Published by Shepherd Works Publishing
Imprint: Shepherd Works Press

Printed in the United States of America

# SERIES PAGE

THE COMMERCIAL REAL ESTATE SYSTEMS SERIES
Structured Thinking for Serious Operators

*The Short Sale*
A Framework for Risk, Negotiation, and Disciplined Resolution

*The Short Sale — Project Workbook*
Short Sale Control System (SSCS)
A Single-Transaction Governance & Execution File

Additional volumes in development.

# DISCLAIMERS & LIMITATION OF LIABILITY

This workbook is provided for informational, structural, and organizational purposes only.

It does not constitute legal, financial, accounting, tax, investment, brokerage, or advisory services.

The author and publisher are not acting as attorneys, financial advisors, accountants, brokers, fiduciaries, or licensed professionals in connection with the use of this workbook.

Distressed property transactions involve material financial risk, legal complexity, and negotiation uncertainty.

Users of this workbook are solely responsible for:

- Independent verification of all assumptions
- Compliance with applicable laws and regulations
- Consultation with qualified licensed professionals
- Evaluation of financial and legal risk
- Capital deployment decisions

No representation or warranty is made regarding:

- Transaction outcomes
- Approval likelihood
- Financial performance
- Risk mitigation effectiveness

Use of this workbook does not create any partnership, joint venture, fiduciary, advisory, agency, or professional services relationship between the user and the author or publisher.

This publication is issued by Shepherd Works Publishing, a Wyoming limited liability company. Nothing in this workbook shall be construed as creating a fiduciary or advisory relationship between the user and the author or publisher.

All advancement decisions, capital authorizations, negotiation strategies, and transaction actions remain solely the responsibility of the Authorized Signatory.

The author and publisher disclaim any liability for loss, claim, or damage arising directly or indirectly from the use of this material.

# DEDICATION

First and always, I give thanks to God the Father, God the Son, and God the Holy Spirit. Every discipline of judgment, restraint, stewardship, and accountability reflected in this system is rooted in the conviction that all authority is ultimately His, and all capital is entrusted, not owned.

To those who practice stewardship over risk, capital, and responsibility with integrity.

To operators who choose discipline over impulse.

To investors who understand that preservation precedes gain.

And to every transaction that demanded restraint before reward.

— James R. Calder

# PREFACE

Distressed transactions rarely fail because of price.

They fail because structure erodes.

Memory replaces documentation.
Momentum replaces discipline.
Assumptions replace verification.

The Short Sale Control System™ was developed to impose order on transactions that are inherently unstable.

A short sale involves multiple stakeholders, compressed timelines, shifting leverage, and material capital exposure. In that environment, informal execution invites error.

Documentation discipline is not administrative excess.

It is risk containment.

A written record:

- Clarifies assumptions
- Exposes weaknesses
- Preserves negotiation leverage
- Protects capital
- Creates accountability

Structured Advancement Authorization prevents drift.
It forces pause before commitment.
It separates analysis from execution.
It distinguishes authority from momentum.

This workbook exists to ensure that distressed transactions are governed — not improvised.

Judgment remains essential.

But judgment must be recorded.

# SYSTEM IDENTIFICATION PAGE

## THE SHORT SALE CONTROL SYSTEM

The Short Sale Control System (SSCS) is a dynamic, phase-based control architecture for managing distressed property transactions with structured reassessment and documented authorization.

This workbook is the execution file of that system.

It does not teach short sales.
It governs their execution.
Each phase concludes with structured advancement authorization.

Movement between phases is deliberate — not automatic.

The project remains the operator's.
The discipline is the system's.

# HOW TO USE THIS WORKBOOK

This workbook is designed for **single-transaction use**.

Each distressed property transaction should have its own dedicated execution file. Do not reuse completed worksheets across multiple transactions.

Proceed sequentially through each phase.

Complete all applicable worksheets before requesting Authorization. Advancement requires documented Authorization by an Authorized Signatory.

If material variables change during execution, regression to an earlier phase is permitted and must be documented.

This workbook is intended to create:

- Documentation discipline
- Risk visibility
- Structured reassessment
- Deliberate authorization
- Transaction accountability

# SELECTING YOUR ROLE PATH

This workbook supports multiple transaction roles.

Each role interacts with the Short Sale Control System™ differently. The structure remains constant, responsibility shifts.

Identify your primary role before proceeding.

You may occupy more than one role. If so, complete all applicable worksheets.

## Primary Transaction Roles

### Investor / Capital Partner

Primary focus:

- Phase II — Feasibility
- Phase III — Structuring
- Phase V — Capital Authorization

Responsibility:

- Net position validation
- Capital exposure approval
- Kill criteria enforcement
- Closing authorization

### Negotiator / Short Sale Specialist

Primary focus:

- Phase III — Structuring
- Phase IV — Execution

Responsibility:

- Submission completeness
- Lender communication control
- Valuation defense
- Concession tracking
- Escalation management

### Operator / Transaction Lead

Primary focus:

- All phases

Responsibility:

- File completeness
- Timeline control
- Risk visibility
- Gate progression
- Documentation integrity

### Authorized Signatory

Primary focus:

- Governance Gates

Selecting Your Role PathResponsibility:

Responsibility:

- Advancement Authorization
- Capital authorization
- Risk acknowledgment
- Conditional approval documentation

No matter what the role:

- The worksheets impose structure.
- The Gates impose pause.
- The Authorized Signatory imposes decision.

# CREATING A COMPLETE AUDIT TRAIL

A distressed transaction should be governable after it is completed.

This workbook is designed to produce a complete execution record.

Every worksheet, log entry, notation, and Gate signature creates a documented sequence of decisions.

An effective audit trail provides:

- Verification of assumptions
- Evidence of structured analysis
- Documentation of risk acknowledgment
- Record of concessions and negotiation posture
- Capital authorization clarity
- Post-closing defensibility

Memory is unreliable.
Momentum distorts recollection.
Documentation preserves fact.

A complete audit trail protects:

- The operator
- The capital partner
- The negotiation posture
- The integrity of future transactions

Each log should be completed contemporaneously.

Each Gate should be signed at the time of authorization.

If regression occurs, it should be documented.

Incomplete documentation weakens governance.

Structured documentation strengthens it.

This workbook is not merely a working file.

It is a transaction record.

# GOVERNANCE GATES WITHIN THE SSCS

The Short Sale Control System (SSCS) incorporates structured authorization gates at defined transition points.

The Short Sale Control System incorporates four formal Gates:

- Gate I — Intake Authorization
- Gate II — Feasibility Authorization
- Gate III — Structuring Authorization
- Gate IV — Capital Deployment

Advancement is not automatic.

Movement between phases requires conscious authorization by an Authorized Signatory.

If deficiencies exist, they must be documented prior to advancement.

The purpose of the Gate structure is not to restrict operator discretion.

It is to require deliberate decision-making.

The project remains yours.

The discipline is the system's.

# DYNAMIC PHASE MODEL OVERVIEW

## DYNAMIC PHASE MODEL

The Short Sale Control System operates in six structured phases:

- Phase I — Intake
- Phase II — Feasibility
- Phase III — Structuring
- Phase IV — Execution
- Phase V — Control & Verification
- Phase VI — Post-Mortem & Refinement

Progression is sequential.

Regression is permitted when material variables change.

Complete worksheets before advancing.

Each Gate should receive a binary authorization:

- Authorize
- Decline
- Conditional Authorization

# WHAT THIS BOOK IS — AND IS NOT

This workbook is a structured transaction governance instrument.

It exists to impose documentation discipline, structured reassessment, and formal advancement authorization on distressed property transactions.

This workbook is:

- An execution control file
- A documentation framework
- A governance architecture
- A risk visibility instrument
- A capital authorization record

This workbook is not:

- • A negotiation training manual
- • A substitute for legal or financial counsel
- • A motivational workbook
- • A theoretical treatise
- • A replacement for professional judgment

The worksheets impose structure.

They do not replace judgment.

The Gates impose pause.

They do not eliminate discretion.

# RECOMMENDED WORKFLOW BY ROLE

While all phases apply to each transaction, emphasis and responsibility vary by role.

Below is a recommended primary workflow emphasis by role.

| Role | Primary Emphasis | Gate Responsibility |
|---|---|---|
| Investor / Capital Partner | Phase II, Phase V | Feasibility Authorization, Capital Authorization |
| Negotiator | Phase III, Phase IV | Submission Control |
| Operator / Transaction Lead | All Phases | File Integrity & Progression Control |
| Authorized Signatory | Governance Gates | Advancement Authorization |

When multiple roles are occupied by the same individual, all applicable responsibilities apply.

No phase is optional.

# TABLE OF CONTENTS

Copyright ........ ii
Series Page ........ iii
Disclaimers & Limitation of Liability ........ iv
Dedication ........ v
Preface ........ vi
System Identification Page ........ vii
How to Use This Workbook ........ viii
Selecting Your Role Path ........ ix
Creating a Complete Audit Trail ........ xi
Governance Gates Within The SSCS ........ xii
Dynamic Phase Model Overview ........ xiii
What This Book Is — And Is Not ........ xiv
Recommended Workflow by Role ........ xv
Table of Contents ........ xvi
Phase I Intake ........ 1
Phase II Feasibilty ........ 41
Phase III Structuring ........ 115
Phase IV Execution ........ 249
Phase V Control & Verification ........ 293
Phase VI Post-Mortem & Refinement ........ 368
Appendix ........ 395

# PHASE I
# INTAKE

# Orientation

**Phase I establishes structural clarity.**

The objective of Intake is to document factual conditions before analysis begins. Assumptions are prohibited in this phase.

This phase records:

- Property condition and occupancy status
- Borrower and seller position
- Distress indicators
- Loan structure and lien hierarchy
- Arrearage and default posture
- Key dates and decision makers
- Initial risk flags

The output of Phase I is a complete factual file.

Advancement beyond this phase requires Intake Authorization by an Authorized Signatory, confirming that material variables have been identified and recorded.

Intake does not evaluate viability.

It defines reality.

***"Reality Precedes Strategy."***

# Project Identification Sheet

Establish foundational transaction identifiers before analysis begins.
Confirm accuracy of all property and loan references prior to proceeding to feasibility review.

## SECTION 1 — PROPERTY IDENTIFICATION

Property Address:

City / State / ZIP:

County:

Parcel Number(s):

Legal Description Reference:

Property Type:

Current Use:

Zoning Classification:

## SECTION 2 — BORROWER INFORMATION

Borrower Name(s):

Entity Type (LLC, LP, Corp, Individual):

Primary Contact:

Phone:

Email:

Phase I
IntakeOccupancy Status:

Occupancy Status:

______________________________________________

- □ Owner Occupied
- □ Tenant Occupied
- □ Vacant

## SECTION 3 — LENDER INFORMATION

Primary Lender / Servicer:

______________________________________________

______________________________________________

Loan Number(s):

______________________________________________

______________________________________________

Original Loan Amount:

______________________________________________

______________________________________________

Current Principal Balance (if known):

______________________________________________

______________________________________________

Customer Service Contact:

______________________________________________

______________________________________________

Loss Mitigation Contact (if known):

______________________________________________

______________________________________________

Portal / Submission Method:

______________________________________________

______________________________________________

## SECTION 4 — INTERNAL FILE CONTROL

Date File Opened:

______________________________________________

______________________________________________

Resolution Operator:

______________________________________________

______________________________________________

Internal File Reference #:

______________________________________________

______________________________________________

Acquisition Strategy (if buyer-side):

______________________________________________

______________________________________________

Phase I
IntakeCapital Source Identified?

Capital Source Identified?

- ☐ Yes
- ☐ No
- ☐ TBD

# Property Profile & Physical Snapshot

Document physical characteristics and observable condition prior to valuation assumptions. Do not rely solely on listing data or borrower representations.

**STRUCTURAL OVERVIEW**

Year Built:

---

Last Major Renovation (if known):

---

Gross Building Area (SF):

---

Net Rentable Area (if applicable):

---

Number of Units / Suites:

---

Construction Type:

---

Roof Type / Condition:

---

Parking Count / Ratio:

---

ADA Compliance Observed:

---

**SITE CHARACTERISTICS**

Lot Size (Acres or SF):

---

Ingress / Egress Points:

---

Corner / Interior / Flag Lot:

---

Topography Issues:

---

Flood Zone (if known):

---

Utility Providers:

Phase I
Intake

______________________________________________

______________________________________________

______________________________________________

Environmental Reports Available?

- □ Yes
- □ No
- □ Unknown

**CONDITION ASSESSMENT**

Deferred Maintenance Observed:

______________________________________________

______________________________________________

______________________________________________

______________________________________________

Capital Improvements Needed (Near Term):

______________________________________________

______________________________________________

______________________________________________

______________________________________________

Structural Concerns Observed:

- □ Known structural issues
- □ Visible cracking / settlement
- □ Roof deterioration
- □ Unknown

Details:

______________________________________________

______________________________________________

______________________________________________

**TENANCY OBSERVATION (If Applicable)**

Tenant Mix Observed:

______________________________________________

Vacancy Observed (Visual Estimate):

______________________________________________

Signage / Exterior Branding Condition:

______________________________________________

______________________________________________

Evidence of Deferred Exterior Maintenance:

______________________________________________

______________________________________________

**DOCUMENTATION AVAILABLE AT INTAKE**

- □ Rent Roll
- □ Trailing 12 Financials
- □ Operating Statement
- □ Appraisal

- □ Environmental Report
- □ Property Condition Report
- □ Survey
- □ Title Report
- □ None Provided

# Borrower / Seller Overview

Assess borrower structure, cooperation likelihood, and decision authority prior to structuring strategy. Document observable behavior and stated motivations without interpretation.

## LEGAL & ENTITY STRUCTURE

Borrower Legal Name:

______________________________________________

Entity Type (LLC, LP, Corp, Individual):

______________________________________________

State of Formation:

______________________________________________

Operating Agreement Reviewed?

- □ Yes
- □ No
- □ Pending

Managing Member / GP Identified:

______________________________________________

Ownership Breakdown (if known):

______________________________________________

Personal Guarantor(s):

______________________________________________

Recourse / Non-Recourse Loan:

______________________________________________

## FINANCIAL POSTURE (AT INTAKE)

Liquidity (Estimated / Stated):

______________________________________________

Other Assets Known:

______________________________________________

Other Liabilities Known:

______________________________________________

Bankruptcy History (if any):

______________________________________________

Active Litigation (if known):

______________________________________________

Tax Delinquencies Known:

- □ Yes
- □ No
- □ Unknown

Details:

______________________________________________

**DISTRESS NARRATIVE**

Borrower's Stated Cause of Distress:

_______________________________________________

_______________________________________________

_______________________________________________

Timeline of Payment Default (if known):

_______________________________________________

Forbearance / Modification Attempts:

_______________________________________________

_______________________________________________

_______________________________________________

Attitude Toward Lender:

- □ Cooperative
- □ Defensive
- □ Hostile
- □ Unknown

Willingness to Provide Documentation:

- □ Immediate
- □ Delayed
- □ Resistant
- □ Unknown

**BEHAVIORAL INDICATORS**

Responsiveness to Communication:

_______________________________________________

Consistency of Information Provided:

_______________________________________________

Emotional State During Discussion:

_______________________________________________

Evidence of Blame-Shifting:

- □ Yes
- □ No
- □ Not Observed

Evidence of Strategic Default:

- □ Yes
- □ No
- □ Unknown

**EXIT OR RESOLUTION POSTURE**

Seller Objective (if stated):

______________________________________________

Time Sensitivity:

______________________________________________

Expectation of Deficiency Waiver:

______________________________________________

Relocation / Transition Needs:

______________________________________________

Other Creditors Involved:

______________________________________________

## Distress Indicator Checklist

Identify objective indicators of financial and structural distress prior to structuring strategy.
Mark only conditions verified through documentation or direct confirmation.

**PAYMENT STATUS**

- □ 30–59 Days Delinquent
- □ 60–89 Days Delinquent
- □ 90+ Days Delinquent
- □ In Forbearance
- □ Performing but Under Stress
- □ Payment History Unknown

Date of Last Confirmed Payment:

Late Fees Accruing?

- □ Yes
- □ No
- □ Unknown

**LOAN STRUCTURE STRESS**

- □ Balloon Payment Within 12 Months
- □ Maturity Default
- □ Interest Rate Reset (Floating / Adjustable)
- □ Debt Service Coverage < 1.0
- □ Negative Cash Flow
- □ Cash Sweep Triggered
- □ Reserve Depletion
- □ Covenant Default
- □ Technical Default
- □ Unknown

Details (if applicable):

**PROPERTY PERFORMANCE DECLINE**

- □ Vacancy Increase > 10%
- □ Tenant Loss (Anchor / Major Tenant)
- □ Rent Concessions Increasing
- □ Operating Expense Spike
- □ Insurance Premium Increase
- □ Property Tax Increase
- □ Deferred Maintenance Escalating
- □ Environmental Issue Identified
- □ Unknown

Narrative (objective observations only):

**CAPITAL STACK PRESSURE**

- □ Junior Lien Present
- □ Mezzanine Debt Present
- □ Preferred Equity Pressure
- □ Personal Guarantees Enforced
- □ Multiple Guarantors Disputing
- □ Cross-Collateralization Exists
- □ Cross-Default Exists
- □ Unknown

Additional Lenders Identified:

## LEGAL / ENFORCEMENT STATUS

□ Notice of Default Filed
□ Acceleration Notice Issued
□ Foreclosure Filed
□ Receiver Appointed
□ UCC Action Initiated
□ Lawsuit Pending
□ Bankruptcy Filed
□ Pre-Foreclosure Discussions Only
□ Unknown

Foreclosure Sale Date (if scheduled): ____________________

Jurisdiction: ____________________

## DISTRESS CONFIRMATION SUMMARY

Primary Distress Driver (Select One):

□ Cash Flow Failure
□ Maturity Default
□ Capital Stack Conflict
□ Market Obsolescence
□ Sponsor Liquidity Failure
□ Legal / Enforcement Trigger
□ Unknown

Secondary Contributing Factors:

____________________

____________________

Is Distress Actionable for Structured Resolution?

□ Yes
□ No
□ Requires Further Verification

Operator Notes (objective only):

____________________

____________________

____________________

# Loan Stack Summary

Document each debt position in order of priority.
Verify balances, maturity, and enforcement status before proceeding to structuring analysis.

**SENIOR DEBT — POSITION 1**

Lender / Servicer:

Loan Type (CMBS, Bank, Agency, Private):

Original Loan Amount:

Current Principal Balance:

Interest Rate / Structure:

Maturity Date:

Amortization Term (if any):

Recourse / Non-Recourse:

Guarantor(s):

Arrearage (if known):

Default Type:

- □ Monetary
- □ Technical
- □ Maturity
- □ Unknown

Enforcement Status:

**JUNIOR DEBT — POSITION 2**

Lender:

Original Loan Amount:

Current Balance:

Interest Rate:

Maturity Date:

Phase I
IntakeRecourse Status:

Recourse Status:

---

Intercreditor Agreement Exists?

- □ Yes
- □ No
- □ Unknown

Standstill / Blockage Provisions Known?

- □ Yes
- □ No
- □ Unknown

Enforcement Status:

---

**MEZZANINE / SUBORDINATED DEBT**

Lender:

---

Current Balance:

---

Interest Structure (Cash / PIK / Hybrid):

---

Maturity Date:

---

UCC Position Filed?

- □ Yes
- □ No
- □ Unknown

Pledge Structure (Equity / Membership Interest):

---

**PREFERRED EQUITY / CAPITAL LAYERS**

Investor Name:

---

Capital Contribution:

---

Preferred Return:

---

Current Accrued Return (if known):

---

Control Rights Triggered?

- □ Yes
- □ No
- □ Unknown

Removal / Replacement Rights:

---

**CROSS-COLLATERALIZATION / CROSS-DEFAULT**

Other Properties Securing Senior Debt:

______________________________________________

______________________________________________

Cross-Default Provisions Identified?

- □ Yes
- □ No
- □ Unknown

Contingent Liabilities Outside Subject Asset:

______________________________________________

______________________________________________

**TOTAL STACK SNAPSHOT**

Total Senior Debt:

______________________________________________

Total Subordinate Debt:

______________________________________________

Total Preferred Equity:

______________________________________________

Estimated All-In Capital Stack:

______________________________________________

Estimated Current As-Is Value (Preliminary):

______________________________________________

Implied Equity Position (Value – Debt):

______________________________________________

**STACK RISK OBSERVATIONS**

Primary Risk Position (Senior / Junior / Mezz / Equity):

______________________________________________

Likely Veto Holder:

______________________________________________

Consent Complexity Level:

- □ Low
- □ Moderate
- □ High

Notes:

______________________________________________

______________________________________________

______________________________________________

# Lien Priority Matrix

Map lien positions in confirmed order of priority.
Do not assume priority without reviewing recorded documents or title evidence.

## LIEN POSITION TABLE

| Position | Lien Holder | Instrument Type | Recording Date | Balance | Enforcement Status |
|---|---|---|---|---|---|
| | | | | | |
| | | | | | |
| | | | | | |
| | | | | | |
| | | | | | |
| | | | | | |
| | | | | | |

## RECORDED ENCUMBRANCES REVIEW

Title Report Reviewed?

- □ Yes
- □ No
- □ Pending

Date of Title Report:

_______________________________________________

Unrecorded Liens Suspected?

- □ Yes
- □ No
- □ Unknown

Details:

_______________________________________________

## INTERCREDITOR STRUCTURE

Intercreditor Agreement Identified?

- □ Yes
- □ No
- □ Unknown

Subordination Agreements Recorded?

- □ Yes
- □ No
- □ Unknown

Standstill Provisions Known?

- □ Yes
- □ No
- □ Unknown

Consent Required from Junior Lienholder?

- □ Yes
- □ No
- □ Unknown

**VETO HOLDER IDENTIFICATION**

Which Position Has Practical Veto Power?

______________________________________________

Which Position Has Economic Leverage?

______________________________________________

Any Position "Out of the Money"?

______________________________________________

Potential Settlement Target:

______________________________________________

**STRUCTURAL RISK NOTES**

Competing Enforcement Actions Possible?

______________________________________________

Foreclosure Priority Clear?

- □ Yes
- □ No
- □ Uncertain

Notes:

______________________________________________

______________________________________________

# Arrearage & Default Summary

Document all arrearages and default-related accruals as of the most recent confirmed date. Verify amounts directly from lender statements when available.

**DEFAULT STATUS OVERVIEW**

Loan Currently in Default?

- □ Yes
- □ No
- □ Unknown

Type of Default:

- □ Monetary
- □ Technical
- □ Maturity
- □ Covenant
- □ Cross-Default
- □ Unknown

Date of Default (if known):

---

Notice of Default Issued?

- □ Yes
- □ No
- □ Unknown

Acceleration Declared?

- □ Yes
- □ No
- □ Unknown

**ARREARAGE BREAKDOWN — SENIOR DEBT**

| **Category** | **Amount** |
|---|---|
| Unpaid Principal | |
| Unpaid Interest | |
| Default Interest | |
| Late Fees | |
| Legal Fees | |
| Protective Advances | |
| Escrow Shortage | |
| Other Charges | |
| Total Arrearage | |

As-Of Date for Above Figures:

---

Source of Figures:

- □ Lender Statement
- □ Verbal Confirmation
- □ Borrower Estimate
- □ Unknown

## JUNIOR / SUBORDINATE ARREARAGE

| Category | Amount |
|---|---|
| Unpaid Principal | |
| Unpaid Interest | |
| Default Interest | |
| Late Fees | |
| Legal Fees | |
| Protective Advances | |
| Escrow Shortage | |
| Other Charges | |
| Total Arrearage | |

If none, include checkbox:

- ☐ No Junior Debt Identified

## MATURITY DEFAULT ANALYSIS

Loan Maturity Date:

___

Balloon Payment Due:

___

Extension Options Remaining?

- ☐ Yes
- ☐ No
- ☐ Unknown

Conditions for Extension:

___

## ACCRUAL VELOCITY

Estimated Monthly Accrual (Interest + Fees):

___

Daily Accrual (if known):

___

Estimated 90-Day Accrual Increase:

___

Does Accrual Worsen LTV Position Materially?

- ☐ Yes
- ☐ No
- ☐ Unknown

## DEFAULT RISK SUMMARY

Primary Economic Pressure Driver:

- ☐ Arrearage Growth
- ☐ Balloon Maturity
- ☐ Legal Costs
- ☐ Default Interest Rate
- ☐ Covenant Trigger
- ☐ Unknown

Phase I
Intake

Time Sensitivity Level:

- □ Low
- □ Moderate
- □ High
- □ Imminent

Operator Observations (objective only):

---

## Occupancy & Income Snapshot

Capture current occupancy and income conditions as of intake date.
Do not substitute projections for verified figures.

**OCCUPANCY STATUS**

Total Units / Suites:

______________________________

Occupied Units / Suites:

______________________________

Vacant Units / Suites:

______________________________

Physical Occupancy %:

______________________________

Economic Occupancy % (if known):

______________________________

Date of Rent Roll (if available):

______________________________

Rent Roll Provided?

- ☐ Yes
- ☐ No
- ☐ Partial

**TENANT MIX SUMMARY**

Major Tenants Identified:

______________________________

______________________________

Anchor Tenant (if applicable):

______________________________

Lease Expirations Within 12 Months:

______________________________

Tenant Concentration Risk Observed:

- ☐ Yes
- ☐ No
- ☐ Unknown

**CURRENT RENTAL INCOME**

| Category | Monthly Amount |
|---|---|
| Gross Potential Rent | |
| Vacancy Loss | |
| Concessions | |
| Other Income | |
| Effective Gross Income | |

As-Of Date:

______________________________

Phase I
IntakeSource of Figures:

Source of Figures:

- □ Rent Roll
- □ T12 Statement
- □ Borrower Estimate
- □ Broker OM
- □ Unknown

**OPERATING EXPENSE SNAPSHOT**

| Expense Category | Monthly Estimate |
|---|---|
| Property Taxes | |
| Insurance | |
| Utilities | |
| Utilities | |
| Repairs & Maintenance | |
| Management | |
| Payroll | |
| Other | |
| Total Operating Expenses | |

Net Operating Income (Current Estimate):

___

Debt Service (Monthly):

___

DSCR (If Calculated):

___

**CASH FLOW CONDITION**

Is Property Currently Cash Flow Positive?

- □ Yes
- □ No
- □ Break-Even
- □ Unknown

Monthly Shortfall (if negative):

___

Trend Direction (Last 6 Months):

- □ Improving
- □ Stable
- □ Declining
- □ Unknown

Primary Income Risk Factor:

___

**SNAPSHOT OBSERVATIONS**

Observed Red Flags:

___

___

Income Verification Gaps:

## Key Contacts & Decision Makers

Identify all parties with decision authority, influence, or veto power.
Do not assume title equals control.

**BORROWER / SPONSOR SIDE**

Primary Decision Maker:

______________________________

Title / Role:

______________________________

Phone:

______________________________

Email:

______________________________

Secondary Decision Maker (if any):

______________________________

Legal Counsel (Borrower):

______________________________

CPA / Financial Advisor:

______________________________

Guarantor Contact (if different):

______________________________

Internal Disputes Observed?

- ☐ Yes
- ☐ No
- ☐ Unknown

Details:

______________________________

**SENIOR LENDER SIDE**

Primary Asset Manager:

______________________________

Direct Phone:

______________________________

Email:

______________________________

Supervisor / Managing Director:

______________________________

Special Assets / Workout Officer:

______________________________

Credit Committee Identified?

- ☐ Yes
- ☐ No
- ☐ Unknown

Internal Approval Required Above Asset Manager?

□ Yes
□ No
□ Unknown

**JUNIOR / SUBORDINATE LENDERS**

Junior Lienholder Contact:

---

Title / Authority Level:

---

Phone / Email:

---

Mezzanine / Equity Representative:

---

Intercreditor Contact (if applicable):

---

**THIRD-PARTY INFLUENCERS**

Receiver (if appointed):

---

Court-Appointed Officer (if any):

---

Bankruptcy Counsel (if applicable):

---

Broker Involved:

---

Property Manager:

---

Title Company Contact:

---

**DECISION AUTHORITY MAPPING**

Who Has Final Approval Authority?

---

Who Has Practical Veto Power?

---

Is There a Hidden Influencer?

---

Is Credit Committee Required?
□ Yes
□ No
□ Unknown

Consent Complexity Level:
□ Low
□ Moderate
□ High

**COMMUNICATION STRATEGY NOTES**

Phase I
IntakePreferred Communication Method (Lender):

Preferred Communication Method (Lender):

___

Response Time Observed:

___

Escalation Path Identified?

___

Notes:

___

___

## Critical Dates & Timeline Tracker

Document all contractual, legal, and operational deadlines affecting resolution.
Update this sheet continuously as new dates are identified.

**CONTRACTUAL DATES**

Original Loan Maturity Date:

---

Extended Maturity Date (if applicable):

---

Next Payment Due Date:

---

Interest Rate Reset Date:

---

Extension Option Deadline:

---

Guaranty Burn-Off Trigger (if any):

---

**DEFAULT & ENFORCEMENT DATES**

Date of First Missed Payment:

---

Notice of Default Date:

---

Acceleration Date:

---

Foreclosure Filing Date:

---

Foreclosure Sale Date (if scheduled):

---

Receiver Appointment Date (if any):

---

Bankruptcy Filing Date (if any):

---

Stay Relief Motion Deadline (if applicable):

---

**LENDER PROCESS TIMELINE**

Short Sale Package Submission Date:

---

Document Deficiency Notice Date:

---

Broker Price Opinion (BPO) Ordered:

---

BPO Inspection Date:

---

Phase I
IntakeAppraisal Ordered:

Appraisal Ordered:

---

Internal Review / Credit Committee Date:

---

Expected Decision Window (Estimated):

---

**THIRD-PARTY DEADLINES**

Title Commitment Date:

---

Environmental Report Date:

---

Lease Expiration (Major Tenant):

---

Insurance Renewal Date:

---

Property Tax Due Date:

---

Utility Cutoff Risk Date (if applicable):

---

**INTERNAL EXECUTION TIMELINE**

Offer Submission Date:

---

Earnest Money Deposit Date:

---

Inspection Period End Date:

---

Financing Commitment Deadline:

---

Closing Target Date:

---

Capital Funding Deadline:

---

**TIMELINE RISK SUMMARY**

Nearest Critical Deadline:

---

Days Remaining to Nearest Deadline:

---

Does Timeline Favor Resolution?

- □ Yes
- □ No
- □ Neutral

Primary Time Pressure Source:

- □ Foreclosure Sale
- □ Balloon Maturity
- □ Accrual Growth
- □ Lease Expiration
- □ Legal Deadline
- □ Other

Operator Notes:

# Initial Risk Flag Register

Identify material risks observed during intake.

Flag only issues that could impair feasibility, structuring, or execution.

**RISK FLAG TABLE**

| Risk Category | Description | Severity (L/M/H) | Impact Area | Mitigation Required | Status |
|---|---|---|---|---|---|
| | | | | | |
| | | | | | |
| | | | | | |
| | | | | | |
| | | | | | |
| | | | | | |
| | | | | | |
| | | | | | |
| | | | | | |
| | | | | | |
| | | | | | |
| | | | | | |

**Suggested Risk Categories**:

- Legal
- Capital Stack
- Title
- Environmental
- Operational
- Tenant
- Behavioral (Borrower)
- Timeline
- Regulatory
- Insurance
- Guarantor
- Consent Complexity

**RISK SCORING SUMMARY**

Total High Severity Flags Identified:

______________________________________________

Is Any Risk Immediately Fatal?

☐ Yes
☐ No
☐ Requires Further Review

Primary Risk Cluster:

______________________________________________

**ESCALATION REQUIREMENT**

Does Any Risk Require:

Credit Committee Pre-Disclosure?

☐ Yes
☐ No

Legal Review Before Offer?

☐ Yes

□ No

Environmental Testing Before Structuring?

□ Yes

□ No

Guarantor Financial Review?

□ Yes

□ No

**STRUCTURED REASSESSMENT TRIGGER**

If any of the following change, Phase I must be revisited:

□ Updated Title Report

□ New Appraisal

□ Bankruptcy Filing

□ Foreclosure Acceleration

□ New Lien Discovered

□ Tenant Departure

□ Material Financial Disclosure

Operator Signature (Optional Discipline Mechanism):

______________________________

Date Reviewed:

______________________________

# Gate I – Intake Authorization

## ADVANCEMENT AUTHORIZATION

Advancement to Phase II — Feasibility is authorized only when Phase I intake data is complete and material risk factors have been identified or documented.
If deficiencies exist, they must be recorded prior to advancement.

## INTAKE CONFIRMATION

Confirm the following:

- □ Property Identification Complete
- □ Borrower / Seller Overview Documented
- □ Distress Indicators Identified
- □ Loan Stack & Lien Priority Confirmed
- □ Arrearage & Default Status Verified
- □ Occupancy & Income Snapshot Recorded
- □ Key Contacts Identified
- □ Critical Dates Logged
- □ Initial Risk Flags Registered

## DEFICIENCIES / NOTATIONS

If any item above is incomplete, document reason and mitigation plan.

______________________________________________________________________

______________________________________________________________________

______________________________________________________________________

## ADVANCEMENT STATUS

- □ Authorized — Advance to Phase II
- □ Authorized with Conditions
- □ Defer Advancement
- □ Do Not Advance

## AUTHORIZED SIGNATORY

Name: ______________________________

Title / Role: ___________________________

Signature: _____________________________

Date: _________________________________

Authority Basis (if applicable):

- □ Sole Operator
- □ Managing Member
- □ General Partner
- □ Investment Committee
- □ Other

## Phase I — Structured Notes

Document observations, tactical considerations, or material developments not captured in structured worksheets.
Maintain objective, execution-focused notation.

# PHASE II
# FEASIBILTY

# Orientation

**Phase II determines whether the transaction supports a defensible net position.**

This phase evaluates:

- Equity position
- Market-supported valuation
- Repair exposure
- Net-to-lender structure
- Capital sufficiency
- Timeline exposure
- Kill criteria thresholds

The objective is not negotiation.

The objective is viability.

Advancement beyond this phase requires Feasibility Authorization by an Authorized Signatory, affirming that risk-adjusted return justifies continued pursuit.

***"Viability Precedes Negotiation."***

# Equity Position Analysis

Determine the subject asset's implied equity position based on verified value inputs and confirmed debt balances.

Use conservative assumptions unless documentation supports otherwise.

**VALUE INPUTS**

Most Recent Appraisal Value (if available):

___

Date of Appraisal:

___

Broker Opinion of Value (BOV):

___

Internal Market Estimate:

___

Selected Working As-Is Value:

___

Basis for Selected Value:

- ☐ Appraisal
- ☐ Broker Opinion
- ☐ Income Approach
- ☐ Comparable Sales
- ☐ Hybrid
- ☐ Other

Rationale for Selected Value:

___

___

___

**TOTAL DEBT POSITION**

Senior Debt Balance:

___

Junior Debt Balance:

___

Mezzanine Debt (if any):

___

Protective Advances / Fees:

___

Total Confirmed Debt:

___

**IMPLIED EQUITY CALCULATION**

| Item | Amount |
|---|---|
| Selected As-Is Value | |
| Total Confirmed Debt | |
| **Implied Equity (Value – Debt)** | |

## EQUITY POSITION STATUS

Is Equity Positive?

- □ Yes
- □ No

If Negative, Estimated Deficiency Amount:

___

Loan-to-Value (Approximate):

___

Is Senior Position Fully Covered by Value?

- □ Yes
- □ No
- □ Borderline

Is Junior Position In the Money?

- □ Yes
- □ No
- □ Partially

## SENSITIVITY CHECK

Value Adjustment Scenario (–5%):

___

Value Adjustment Scenario (–10%):

___

Does Minor Value Shift Eliminate Equity?

- □ Yes
- □ No

Is Equity Margin Structurally Thin?

- □ Yes
- □ No

## FEASIBILITY SIGNAL

Short Sale Feasible Based on Equity Position?

- □ Yes — Economic Rationale Clear
- □ Yes — But Thin Margin
- □ Uncertain — Requires Further Validation
- □ No — Equity Present

Primary Economic Constraint:

___

Operator Notes:

___

___

___

# Market Value Estimation Worksheet

Estimate current market value using applicable valuation methods.
Document assumptions and reconcile variances before selecting a working value.

**SALES COMPARISON APPROACH**

Number of Comparable Sales Reviewed:

___

Average Sale Price per SF:

___

Subject Property Size (SF):

___

Indicated Value (Sales Comparison):

___

Adjustments Applied (if any):

___

___

Confidence Level:

- □ High
- □ Moderate
- □ Low

**INCOME APPROACH**

Current NOI (Verified or Estimated):

___

Market Cap Rate Applied:

___

Indicated Value (NOI ÷ Cap Rate):

___

Cap Rate Source:

- □ Market Survey
- □ Broker Input
- □ Recent Comps
- □ Internal Estimate

Adjustments / Normalizations:

___

___

Confidence Level:

- □ High
- □ Moderate
- □ Low

**COST APPROACH (If Applicable)**

Land Value Estimate:

___

Replacement Cost (Improvements):

___

Phase II
FeasibiltyLess Depreciation:

Less Depreciation:

---

Indicated Value (Cost Approach):

---

Confidence Level:

- □ High
- □ Moderate
- □ Low

## VALUE RECONCILIATION

Highest Indicated Value:

---

Lowest Indicated Value:

---

Spread Between Methods:

---

Primary Method Relied Upon:

- □ Sales Comparison
- □ Income Approach
- □ Cost Approach
- □ Hybrid

Selected Working As-Is Value:

---

Rationale for Final Selection:

---

---

## MARKET CONDITION ADJUSTMENT

Current Market Direction:

- □ Appreciating
- □ Stable
- □ Softening
- □ Declining

Time on Market Trend:

---

Liquidity Assessment:

- □ High
- □ Moderate
- □ Low

Is Selected Value Aggressive?

- □ Yes
- □ No

Is Selected Value Defensive?

- □ Yes
- □ No

**VALUATION RISK SUMMARY**

Primary Valuation Risk:

______________________________________________

Sensitivity to Cap Rate Shift (±0.5%):

______________________________________________

Would a Lender Challenge This Value?

- □ Likely
- □ Possible
- □ Unlikely

Operator Notes:

______________________________________________

______________________________________________

______________________________________________

# Comparable Sales Log

Document each comparable sale reviewed in support of value analysis.

Record objective data and material differences **without narrative bias.**

**COMPARABLE SALE — ENTRY**

Comparable Property Address:

______________________________

City / Submarket:

______________________________

Property Type:

______________________________

Sale Date:

______________________________

Sale Price:

______________________________

Sale Price per SF / Unit:

______________________________

Building Size (SF):

______________________________

Lot Size (if relevant):

______________________________

Year Built:

______________________________

Condition at Sale:

______________________________

Occupancy at Sale:

______________________________

Cap Rate (if known):

______________________________

Buyer Type (Private, Institutional, Owner-User):

______________________________

Source of Data:

- □ MLS
- □ CoStar
- □ Broker
- □ Public Record
- □ Other

Verification Level:

- □ Confirmed Public Record
- □ Broker Confirmed
- □ Unverified

**ADJUSTMENT FACTORS**

Location Superiority / Inferiority:

Size Differential Adjustment:

Condition Adjustment:

Income Differential:

Time Adjustment (Market Movement):

Other Adjustments:

Adjusted Indicated Value per SF:

Adjusted Indicated Total Value:

**COMPARABLE QUALITY ASSESSMENT**

Similarity to Subject:

- □ High
- □ Moderate
- □ Low

Primary Strength of This Comparable:

Primary Weakness of This Comparable:

Would a Lender Rely on This Comp?

- □ Likely
- □ Possible
- □ Unlikely

**OPERATOR NOTES**

Observations:

# Comparable Sales Log

Document each comparable sale reviewed in support of value analysis.

Record objective data and material differences **without narrative bias.**

**COMPARABLE SALE — ENTRY**

Comparable Property Address:

______________________________

City / Submarket:

______________________________

Property Type:

______________________________

Sale Date:

______________________________

Sale Price:

______________________________

Sale Price per SF / Unit:

______________________________

Building Size (SF):

______________________________

Lot Size (if relevant):

______________________________

Year Built:

______________________________

Condition at Sale:

______________________________

Occupancy at Sale:

______________________________

Cap Rate (if known):

______________________________

Buyer Type (Private, Institutional, Owner-User):

______________________________

Source of Data:

- □ MLS
- □ CoStar
- □ Broker
- □ Public Record
- □ Other

Verification Level:

- □ Confirmed Public Record
- □ Broker Confirmed
- □ Unverified

**ADJUSTMENT FACTORS**

Location Superiority / Inferiority:

Size Differential Adjustment:

Condition Adjustment:

Income Differential:

Time Adjustment (Market Movement):

Other Adjustments:

Adjusted Indicated Value per SF:

Adjusted Indicated Total Value:

**COMPARABLE QUALITY ASSESSMENT**

Similarity to Subject:

□ High
□ Moderate
□ Low

Primary Strength of This Comparable:

Primary Weakness of This Comparable:

Would a Lender Rely on This Comp?

□ Likely
□ Possible
□ Unlikely

**OPERATOR NOTES**

Observations:

# Comparable Sales Log

Document each comparable sale reviewed in support of value analysis.

Record objective data and material differences **without narrative bias.**

**COMPARABLE SALE — ENTRY**

Comparable Property Address:

______________________________

City / Submarket:

______________________________

Property Type:

______________________________

Sale Date:

______________________________

Sale Price:

______________________________

Sale Price per SF / Unit:

______________________________

Building Size (SF):

______________________________

Lot Size (if relevant):

______________________________

Year Built:

______________________________

Condition at Sale:

______________________________

Occupancy at Sale:

______________________________

Cap Rate (if known):

______________________________

Buyer Type (Private, Institutional, Owner-User):

______________________________

Source of Data:

- ☐ MLS
- ☐ CoStar
- ☐ Broker
- ☐ Public Record
- ☐ Other

Verification Level:

- ☐ Confirmed Public Record
- ☐ Broker Confirmed
- ☐ Unverified

**ADJUSTMENT FACTORS**

Location Superiority / Inferiority:

Size Differential Adjustment:

Condition Adjustment:

Income Differential:

Time Adjustment (Market Movement):

Other Adjustments:

Adjusted Indicated Value per SF:

Adjusted Indicated Total Value:

**COMPARABLE QUALITY ASSESSMENT**

Similarity to Subject:

- □ High
- □ Moderate
- □ Low

Primary Strength of This Comparable:

Primary Weakness of This Comparable:

Would a Lender Rely on This Comp?

- □ Likely
- □ Possible
- □ Unlikely

**OPERATOR NOTES**

Observations:

# Comparable Sales Log

Document each comparable sale reviewed in support of value analysis.

Record objective data and material differences **without narrative bias.**

**COMPARABLE SALE — ENTRY**

Comparable Property Address:

______________________________________________

City / Submarket:

______________________________________________

Property Type:

______________________________________________

Sale Date:

______________________________________________

Sale Price:

______________________________________________

Sale Price per SF / Unit:

______________________________________________

Building Size (SF):

______________________________________________

Lot Size (if relevant):

______________________________________________

Year Built:

______________________________________________

Condition at Sale:

______________________________________________

Occupancy at Sale:

______________________________________________

Cap Rate (if known):

______________________________________________

Buyer Type (Private, Institutional, Owner-User):

______________________________________________

Source of Data:

- □ MLS
- □ CoStar
- □ Broker
- □ Public Record
- □ Other

Verification Level:

- □ Confirmed Public Record
- □ Broker Confirmed
- □ Unverified

**ADJUSTMENT FACTORS**

Location Superiority / Inferiority:

Size Differential Adjustment:

Condition Adjustment:

Income Differential:

Time Adjustment (Market Movement):

Other Adjustments:

Adjusted Indicated Value per SF:

Adjusted Indicated Total Value:

## COMPARABLE QUALITY ASSESSMENT

Similarity to Subject:

- □ High
- □ Moderate
- □ Low

Primary Strength of This Comparable:

Primary Weakness of This Comparable:

Would a Lender Rely on This Comp?

- □ Likely
- □ Possible
- □ Unlikely

## OPERATOR NOTES

Observations:

# Comparable Sales Log

Document each comparable sale reviewed in support of value analysis.

Record objective data and material differences **without narrative bias.**

**COMPARABLE SALE — ENTRY**

Comparable Property Address:

---

City / Submarket:

---

Property Type:

---

Sale Date:

---

Sale Price:

---

Sale Price per SF / Unit:

---

Building Size (SF):

---

Lot Size (if relevant):

---

Year Built:

---

Condition at Sale:

---

Occupancy at Sale:

---

Cap Rate (if known):

---

Buyer Type (Private, Institutional, Owner-User):

---

Source of Data:

- □ MLS
- □ CoStar
- □ Broker
- □ Public Record
- □ Other

Verification Level:

- □ Confirmed Public Record
- □ Broker Confirmed
- □ Unverified

**ADJUSTMENT FACTORS**

Location Superiority / Inferiority:

---

Size Differential Adjustment:

---

Condition Adjustment:

---

Income Differential:

---

Time Adjustment (Market Movement):

---

Other Adjustments:

---

Adjusted Indicated Value per SF:

---

Adjusted Indicated Total Value:

---

**COMPARABLE QUALITY ASSESSMENT**

Similarity to Subject:

- □ High
- □ Moderate
- □ Low

Primary Strength of This Comparable:

---

Primary Weakness of This Comparable:

---

Would a Lender Rely on This Comp?

- □ Likely
- □ Possible
- □ Unlikely

**OPERATOR NOTES**

Observations:

---

---

---

# Comparable Sales Log

Document each comparable sale reviewed in support of value analysis.

Record objective data and material differences **without narrative bias.**

**COMPARABLE SALE — ENTRY**

Comparable Property Address:

______________________________

City / Submarket:

______________________________

Property Type:

______________________________

Sale Date:

______________________________

Sale Price:

______________________________

Sale Price per SF / Unit:

______________________________

Building Size (SF):

______________________________

Lot Size (if relevant):

______________________________

Year Built:

______________________________

Condition at Sale:

______________________________

Occupancy at Sale:

______________________________

Cap Rate (if known):

______________________________

Buyer Type (Private, Institutional, Owner-User):

______________________________

Source of Data:

- □ MLS
- □ CoStar
- □ Broker
- □ Public Record
- □ Other

Verification Level:

- □ Confirmed Public Record
- □ Broker Confirmed
- □ Unverified

**ADJUSTMENT FACTORS**

Location Superiority / Inferiority:

Size Differential Adjustment:

Condition Adjustment:

Income Differential:

Time Adjustment (Market Movement):

Other Adjustments:

Adjusted Indicated Value per SF:

Adjusted Indicated Total Value:

## COMPARABLE QUALITY ASSESSMENT

Similarity to Subject:

- ☐ High
- ☐ Moderate
- ☐ Low

Primary Strength of This Comparable:

Primary Weakness of This Comparable:

Would a Lender Rely on This Comp?

- ☐ Likely
- ☐ Possible
- ☐ Unlikely

## OPERATOR NOTES

Observations:

## Comparable Sales Log

Document each comparable sale reviewed in support of value analysis.

Record objective data and material differences **without narrative bias.**

### COMPARABLE SALE — ENTRY

Comparable Property Address:

_______________________________________________

City / Submarket:

_______________________________________________

Property Type:

_______________________________________________

Sale Date:

_______________________________________________

Sale Price:

_______________________________________________

Sale Price per SF / Unit:

_______________________________________________

Building Size (SF):

_______________________________________________

Lot Size (if relevant):

_______________________________________________

Year Built:

_______________________________________________

Condition at Sale:

_______________________________________________

Occupancy at Sale:

_______________________________________________

Cap Rate (if known):

_______________________________________________

Buyer Type (Private, Institutional, Owner-User):

_______________________________________________

Source of Data:

- □ MLS
- □ CoStar
- □ Broker
- □ Public Record
- □ Other

Verification Level:

- □ Confirmed Public Record
- □ Broker Confirmed
- □ Unverified

### ADJUSTMENT FACTORS

Location Superiority / Inferiority:

Size Differential Adjustment:

Condition Adjustment:

Income Differential:

Time Adjustment (Market Movement):

Other Adjustments:

Adjusted Indicated Value per SF:

Adjusted Indicated Total Value:

**COMPARABLE QUALITY ASSESSMENT**

Similarity to Subject:

- □ High
- □ Moderate
- □ Low

Primary Strength of This Comparable:

Primary Weakness of This Comparable:

Would a Lender Rely on This Comp?

- □ Likely
- □ Possible
- □ Unlikely

**OPERATOR NOTES**

Observations:

# Comparable Sales Log

Document each comparable sale reviewed in support of value analysis.

Record objective data and material differences **without narrative bias.**

**COMPARABLE SALE — ENTRY**

Comparable Property Address:

City / Submarket:

Property Type:

Sale Date:

Sale Price:

Sale Price per SF / Unit:

Building Size (SF):

Lot Size (if relevant):

Year Built:

Condition at Sale:

Occupancy at Sale:

Cap Rate (if known):

Buyer Type (Private, Institutional, Owner-User):

Source of Data:

- □ MLS
- □ CoStar
- □ Broker
- □ Public Record
- □ Other

Verification Level:

- □ Confirmed Public Record
- □ Broker Confirmed
- □ Unverified

**ADJUSTMENT FACTORS**

Location Superiority / Inferiority:

Size Differential Adjustment:

Condition Adjustment:

Income Differential:

Time Adjustment (Market Movement):

Other Adjustments:

Adjusted Indicated Value per SF:

Adjusted Indicated Total Value:

## COMPARABLE QUALITY ASSESSMENT

Similarity to Subject:

- □ High
- □ Moderate
- □ Low

Primary Strength of This Comparable:

Primary Weakness of This Comparable:

Would a Lender Rely on This Comp?

- □ Likely
- □ Possible
- □ Unlikely

## OPERATOR NOTES

Observations:

# Comparable Sales Log

Document each comparable sale reviewed in support of value analysis.

Record objective data and material differences **without narrative bias.**

**COMPARABLE SALE — ENTRY**

Comparable Property Address:

---

City / Submarket:

---

Property Type:

---

Sale Date:

---

Sale Price:

---

Sale Price per SF / Unit:

---

Building Size (SF):

---

Lot Size (if relevant):

---

Year Built:

---

Condition at Sale:

---

Occupancy at Sale:

---

Cap Rate (if known):

---

Buyer Type (Private, Institutional, Owner-User):

---

Source of Data:

- □ MLS
- □ CoStar
- □ Broker
- □ Public Record
- □ Other

Verification Level:

- □ Confirmed Public Record
- □ Broker Confirmed
- □ Unverified

**ADJUSTMENT FACTORS**

Location Superiority / Inferiority:

Size Differential Adjustment:

Condition Adjustment:

Income Differential:

Time Adjustment (Market Movement):

Other Adjustments:

Adjusted Indicated Value per SF:

Adjusted Indicated Total Value:

## COMPARABLE QUALITY ASSESSMENT

Similarity to Subject:

- □ High
- □ Moderate
- □ Low

Primary Strength of This Comparable:

Primary Weakness of This Comparable:

Would a Lender Rely on This Comp?

- □ Likely
- □ Possible
- □ Unlikely

## OPERATOR NOTES

Observations:

# Comparable Sales Log

Document each comparable sale reviewed in support of value analysis.

Record objective data and material differences **without narrative bias.**

**COMPARABLE SALE — ENTRY**

Comparable Property Address:

City / Submarket:

Property Type:

Sale Date:

Sale Price:

Sale Price per SF / Unit:

Building Size (SF):

Lot Size (if relevant):

Year Built:

Condition at Sale:

Occupancy at Sale:

Cap Rate (if known):

Buyer Type (Private, Institutional, Owner-User):

Source of Data:

- ☐ MLS
- ☐ CoStar
- ☐ Broker
- ☐ Public Record
- ☐ Other

Verification Level:

- ☐ Confirmed Public Record
- ☐ Broker Confirmed
- ☐ Unverified

**ADJUSTMENT FACTORS**

Location Superiority / Inferiority:

Size Differential Adjustment:

Condition Adjustment:

Income Differential:

Time Adjustment (Market Movement):

Other Adjustments:

Adjusted Indicated Value per SF:

Adjusted Indicated Total Value:

**COMPARABLE QUALITY ASSESSMENT**

Similarity to Subject:

- □ High
- □ Moderate
- □ Low

Primary Strength of This Comparable:

Primary Weakness of This Comparable:

Would a Lender Rely on This Comp?

- □ Likely
- □ Possible
- □ Unlikely

**OPERATOR NOTES**

Observations:

# Repair & Deferred Maintenance Estimate

Document observable deferred maintenance and required capital improvements.
Base estimates on contractor input, prior reports, or conservative assumptions.

## DEFERRED MAINTENANCE ITEMS

| Item Description | Category | Estimated Cost | Verification Level |
|---|---|---|---|
| | | | □ Contractor Quote<br>□ Engineer Report<br>□ Visual Estimate<br>□ Borrower Stated<br>□ Unknown |
| | | | □ Contractor Quote<br>□ Engineer Report<br>□ Visual Estimate<br>□ Borrower Stated<br>□ Unknown |
| | | | □ Contractor Quote<br>□ Engineer Report<br>□ Visual Estimate<br>□ Borrower Stated<br>□ Unknown |
| | | | □ Contractor Quote<br>□ Engineer Report<br>□ Visual Estimate<br>□ Borrower Stated<br>□ Unknown |
| | | | □ Contractor Quote<br>□ Engineer Report<br>□ Visual Estimate<br>□ Borrower Stated<br>□ Unknown |
| | | | □ Contractor Quote<br>□ Engineer Report<br>□ Visual Estimate<br>□ Borrower Stated<br>□ Unknown |
| | | | □ Contractor Quote<br>□ Engineer Report<br>□ Visual Estimate<br>□ Borrower Stated<br>□ Unknown |
| | | | □ Contractor Quote<br>□ Engineer Report<br>□ Visual Estimate<br>□ Borrower Stated<br>□ Unknown |
| | | | □ Contractor Quote<br>□ Engineer Report<br>□ Visual Estimate<br>□ Borrower Stated<br>□ Unknown |

**Suggested Categories:**

- Roof
- HVAC
- Structural
- Electrical
- Plumbing
- Interior
- Exterior
- Environmental

- Life Safety
- Parking / Paving
- ADA Compliance

## CAPITAL IMPROVEMENT REQUIREMENTS

| Improvement | Timing (Immediate / 12mo / 24mo) | Estimated Cost | Impact on Value |
|---|---|---|---|
| | | | |
| | | | |
| | | | |
| | | | |
| | | | |
| | | | |
| | | | |
| | | | |
| | | | |
| | | | |

## TOTAL ESTIMATED COST SUMMARY

| Category | Amount |
|---|---|
| Immediate Repairs | |
| Near-Term Capital (12 Months) | |
| Long-Term Capital (24+ Months) | |
| Total Estimated Capital Requirement | |

## VALUE IMPACT ANALYSIS

Does Deferred Maintenance Materially Affect As-Is Value?

□ Yes
□ No

Estimated Value Adjustment Due to Condition:

___

Is Lender Likely to Commission Their Own Inspection?

□ Yes
□ No
□ Likely

Would a BPO Reflect These Deficiencies?

□ Yes
□ No
□ Uncertain

## LIQUIDITY IMPACT

Does Condition Reduce Buyer Pool?

□ Yes
□ No

Estimated Buyer Type Most Likely:

□ Investor
□ Owner-User

Phase II
Feasibilty□ Opportunistic

□ Opportunistic
□ Distressed Specialist

Does Condition Increase Timeline Risk?

□ Yes
□ No

**OPERATOR NOTES**

Supporting Documentation Attached?

□ Yes
□ No

Observations:

___

___

___

## Net-to-Lender Feasibility Model

Compare estimated lender recovery under a short sale versus foreclosure scenario.
Use conservative assumptions and document sources where available.

**SHORT SALE RECOVERY SCENARIO**

Proposed Purchase Price:

______________________________

Less: Closing Costs (Title, Escrow, etc.):

______________________________

Less: Broker Commission (if applicable):

______________________________

Less: Unpaid Taxes / Liens:

______________________________

Less: Repair Credits / Concessions:

______________________________

Less: Legal / Workout Fees:

______________________________

Estimated Net to Senior Lender:

______________________________

Junior Payoff Allocation (if any):

______________________________

Net to Junior (if applicable):

______________________________

Insert structured summary table:

| Item | Amount |
|---|---|
| Gross Sales Price | |
| Total Deductions | |
| Net Recovery (Short Sale) | |

**FORECLOSURE RECOVERY SCENARIO**

Estimated Foreclosure Sale Value:

______________________________

Less: Foreclosure Legal Costs:

______________________________

Less: Carry Costs (Taxes, Insurance, Utilities):

______________________________

Less: Property Management / REO Costs:

______________________________

Less: Repair / Stabilization Costs:

______________________________

Less: Market Time Carry (Interest Accrual):

______________________________

Estimated Net After Foreclosure:

______________________________

Phase II
FeasibiltyEstimated Timeline to Liquidation (Months):

Estimated Timeline to Liquidation (Months):

| Item | Amount |
|---|---|
| Estimated REO Value | |
| Total Foreclosure Costs | |
| Net Recovery (Foreclosure) | |

**RECOVERY COMPARISON**

Net Short Sale Recovery:

---

Net Foreclosure Recovery:

---

Recovery Differential (Short Sale – Foreclosure):

---

Short Sale Economically Superior?

- □ Yes
- □ No
- □ Marginal

If No, Primary Constraint:

---

**DEFICIENCY POSITION**

Total Debt Balance:

---

Short Sale Deficiency Amount:

---

Foreclosure Deficiency Amount:

---

Guarantor Collectability (Preliminary):

- □ High
- □ Moderate
- □ Low
- □ Unknown

Does Deficiency Recovery Influence Lender Decision?

- □ Yes
- □ No
- □ Likely

## FEASIBILITY CONCLUSION

Is There a Clear Economic Case for Short Sale?

- □ Yes — Superior Recovery
- □ Yes — Lower Risk
- □ Marginal
- □ No

Primary Argument to Lender:

______________________________________________________________________

Secondary Leverage Points:

______________________________________________________________________

Operator Notes:

______________________________________________________________________

______________________________________________________________________

# Offer Structuring Matrix

Evaluate alternative offer structures prior to submission.
Compare economic impact, risk allocation, and lender acceptance probability.

## STRUCTURE OPTIONS COMPARISON

| Structure Element | Option A | Option B | Option C | Notes |
|---|---|---|---|---|
| Purchase Price | | | | |
| Earnest Money | | | | |
| Inspection Period | | | | |
| Closing Timeline | | | | |
| Cash at Closing | | | | |
| Seller Contribution | | | | |
| Repair Credits | | | | |
| Tax Proration Structure | | | | |
| Commission Structure | | | | |

| Structure Element | Option A | Option B | Option C | Notes |
|---|---|---|---|---|
| Junior Lien Settlement | | | | |
| Deficiency Treatment | | | | |
| Guarantor Release | | | | |
| Escrow Holdback | | | | |
| Financing Contingency | | | | |
| Assignment Rights | | | | |
| Other Concessions | | | | |

**Notes:**

## ECONOMIC IMPACT ANALYSIS

Which Option Maximizes Net to Lender?

Which Option Maximizes Acceptance Probability?

Which Option Minimizes Execution Risk?

Most Balanced Option:

## LENDER ACCEPTANCE PROBABILITY

Option A — Acceptance Probability:

- □ High
- □ Moderate
- □ Low

Option B — Acceptance Probability:

- □ High
- □ Moderate
- □ Low

Option C — Acceptance Probability:

- □ High
- □ Moderate
- □ Low

Primary Anticipated Objection:

______________________________________________

Mitigation Strategy:

______________________________________________

## RISK ALLOCATION REVIEW

Which Option Places More Risk on Buyer?

______________________________________________

Which Option Shifts Risk to Lender?

______________________________________________

Which Option Reduces Timeline Risk?

______________________________________________

Is Any Option Structurally Aggressive?

- □ Yes
- □ No

## NEGOTIATION POSITIONING

Opening Position Selected:

- □ Option A
- □ Option B
- □ Option C

Fallback Structure Identified?

- □ Yes
- □ No

Escalation Strategy if Rejected:

______________________________________________

______________________________________________

Operator Notes:

______________________________________________

______________________________________________

______________________________________________

# Capital Stack Planning Sheet

Define the capital structure required to execute the proposed acquisition.
Document sources, terms, and contingencies prior to offer submission.

**USES OF FUNDS**

| **Use Category** | **Amount** |
|---|---|
| Purchase Price | |
| Closing Costs | |
| Due Diligence Costs | |
| Repair / Immediate Capital | |
| Working Capital Reserve | |
| Financing Costs | |
| Contingency Reserve | |
| Other | |
| Total Uses of Funds | |

**SOURCES OF FUNDS**

| **Source** | **Amount** |
|---|---|
| Equity — Sponsor | |
| Equity — Investors | |
| Senior Acquisition Loan | |
| Seller Financing | |
| Mezzanine Debt | |
| Preferred Equity | |
| Bridge Loan | |
| Other | |
| Total Sources of Funds | |

**CAPITAL STRUCTURE BREAKDOWN**

Loan-to-Cost (Estimated):

___

Loan-to-Value (Estimated):

___

Equity Contribution %:

___

Debt Service Coverage (Projected):

___

Is Capital Stack Fully Funded?

- □ Yes
- □ No
- □ Pending Commitments

**EQUITY STRUCTURE**

Sponsor Equity Contribution:

Outside Investor Equity:

Preferred Return (if applicable):

Equity Split Structure:

Control Rights:

Capital Call Provisions Identified?
- □ Yes
- □ No

**FINANCING STRUCTURE**

Lender Identified?
- □ Yes
- □ No

Loan Type:

Interest Rate (Estimated):

Term Length:

Amortization:

Recourse Structure:

Financing Contingency Required?
- □ Yes
- □ No

**FUNDING RISK ASSESSMENT**

Primary Capital Risk:

Is Equity Soft or Verbal Only?
- □ Yes
- □ No

Is Debt Commitment Formal?
- □ Yes
- □ No

□ Term Sheet Only

Sensitivity to Interest Rate Shift:

Does Capital Stack Allow for Repair Budget?
- □ Yes
- □ No

**EXECUTION CONFIDENCE**

Capital Stack Stability Level:

- □ Strong
- □ Moderate
- □ Weak

Is Offer Submission Premature Based on Capital?

- □ Yes
- □ No

Operator Notes:

______________________________________________

______________________________________________

______________________________________________

# Cash Requirement & Liquidity Review

Assess total cash requirements and confirm sufficient liquidity for acquisition, stabilization, and contingency. Document verified liquidity sources prior to submission.

**ACQUISITION CASH REQUIREMENTS**

Earnest Money Deposit:

Initial Due Diligence Costs:

Equity at Closing:

Closing Cost Cash Portion:

Immediate Repair Funding Required:

Initial Operating Reserve Required:

Total Immediate Cash Requirement:

**POST-CLOSING OPERATING RUNWAY**

Projected Monthly Debt Service:

Projected Monthly Operating Expense:

Projected Monthly Net Shortfall (if any):

Required Operating Reserve (Months):

Total Stabilization Reserve Required:

**SPONSOR LIQUIDITY POSITION**

Cash on Hand (Verified):

Available Credit Lines:

Committed Investor Capital (Hard):

Verbal / Soft Commitments:

Other Liquid Assets Available:

Total Verified Liquidity:

---

**LIQUIDITY GAP ANALYSIS**

Total Immediate Cash Requirement:

---

Total Verified Liquidity:

---

Liquidity Surplus / Shortfall:

---

Is Liquidity Adequate?

- □ Yes
- □ Marginal
- □ No

**STRESS LIQUIDITY TEST**

If Repairs Increase by 10%:

---

If Lease-Up Delays by 6 Months:

---

If Financing Terms Worsen:

---

Does Sponsor Remain Solvent Under Stress?

- □ Yes
- □ No
- □ Uncertain

**PERSONAL GUARANTEE RISK (If Applicable)**

Is Recourse Exposure Present?

- □ Yes
- □ No

Estimated Personal Exposure:

---

Would Shortfall Trigger Personal Asset Risk?

- □ Yes
- □ No

**EXECUTION CONFIDENCE**

Liquidity Stability Level:

- □ Strong
- □ Moderate
- □ Fragile

Is Capital Stack Over-Levered?

- □ Yes
- □ No

Operator Notes:

Phase II
Feasibilty

# Exit Strategy Planner

Define primary and secondary exit strategies prior to acquisition.
Document timeline assumptions, performance triggers, and capital return targets.

## PRIMARY EXIT STRATEGY

Primary Exit Type:

- □ Sale
- □ Refinance
- □ Hold for Cash Flow
- □ Redevelopment & Disposition
- □ 1031 Exchange
- □ Other

Target Holding Period (Years):

___

Projected Stabilized NOI:

___

Target Exit Cap Rate:

___

Projected Exit Value:

___

Remaining Debt at Exit:

___

Projected Net Sale Proceeds:

___

Target Equity Multiple:

___

Target IRR (if applicable):

___

## SECONDARY / CONTINGENCY EXIT

Alternate Exit Strategy:

___

Trigger for Alternate Strategy:

___

Revised Holding Period:

___

Revised Performance Target:

___

## PERFORMANCE MILESTONES

Stabilization Target Date:

___

Occupancy Target %:

___

Rent Growth Target:

___

Expense Ratio Target:

___

Phase II
Feasibilty

Refinance Qualification Metrics:

---

## MARKET EXIT RISK

Market Liquidity Assessment:

- □ High
- □ Moderate
- □ Low

Cap Rate Expansion Risk:

- □ High
- □ Moderate
- □ Low

Interest Rate Sensitivity:

---

Buyer Pool at Exit:

- □ Institutional
- □ Private Investor
- □ Owner-User
- □ Opportunistic

## VALUE CREATION PLAN

Primary Value Drivers:

---

---

Operational Improvements Planned:

---

Capital Improvements Planned:

---

Lease-Up Strategy:

---

## FAILURE SCENARIO PLANNING

If Stabilization Delayed 12 Months:

---

If NOI Underperforms by 10%:

---

If Exit Cap Rate Expands by 1%:

---

Is Exit Strategy Still Viable Under Stress?

- □ Yes
- □ No
- □ Marginal

## STRATEGIC ALIGNMENT

Does Exit Align With Investor Time Horizon?

- □ Yes
- □ No

Does Exit Align With Financing Term?

- □ Yes
- □ No

Does Exit Align With Liquidity Plan?

- □ Yes
- □ No

Operator Notes:

______________________________________________________________________________

______________________________________________________________________________

______________________________________________________________________________

# Scenario Stress Test Worksheet

Evaluate downside scenarios and assess impact on value, liquidity, and exit viability.
Document whether capital structure remains stable under stress.

**BASELINE ASSUMPTIONS**

Baseline As-Is Value:

---

Baseline Stabilized NOI:

---

Baseline Cap Rate:

---

Baseline Exit Value:

---

Baseline Debt Service:

---

Baseline Liquidity Reserve:

---

**SCENARIO 1 — NOI REDUCTION**

NOI Decrease Assumed:

- □ –5%
- □ –10%
- □ –15%
- □ Other

Revised NOI:

---

Revised Value (Income Approach):

---

Revised DSCR:

---

Impact on Exit Value:

---

Is Project Still Viable?

- □ Yes
- □ Marginal
- □ No

**SCENARIO 2 — CAP RATE EXPANSION**

Cap Rate Increase Assumed:

- □ +0.5%
- □ +1.0%
- □ +1.5%
- □ Other

Revised Exit Value:

---

Phase II
FeasibiltyEquity Reduction:

Equity Reduction:

---

Revised Equity Multiple:

---

Is Exit Strategy Still Achievable?

- □ Yes
- □ Marginal
- □ No

**SCENARIO 3 — REPAIR COST OVERRUN**

Repair Cost Increase Assumed:

- □ +5%
- □ +10%
- □ +20%
- □ Other

Revised Total Capital Required:

---

Liquidity Surplus / Shortfall:

---

Requires Additional Equity?

- □ Yes
- □ No

**SCENARIO 4 — LEASE-UP DELAY**

Lease-Up Delay Assumed:

- □ 3 Months
- □ 6 Months
- □ 12 Months
- □ Other

Additional Carry Cost:

---

Revised Liquidity Position:

---

Impact on Refinance Timeline:

---

**SCENARIO 5 — INTEREST RATE INCREASE**

Rate Increase Assumed:

- □ +50 bps
- □ +100 bps
- □ +150 bps
- □ Other

Revised Debt Service:

---

Revised DSCR:

---

Refinance Risk Increased?

- □ Yes
- □ No

**COMBINED DOWNSIDE CASE**

Worst-Case Scenario Modeled:

---

Revised Equity Position:

---

Revised IRR:

---

Does Capital Stack Collapse?

- □ Yes
- □ No
- □ Borderline

**STRESS RESILIENCE SUMMARY**

Strongest Vulnerability:

---

Most Likely Downside Scenario:

---

Does Sponsor Remain Solvent Under Combined Stress?

- □ Yes
- □ No

Is Offer Price Still Justified Under Stress?

- □ Yes
- □ No

Operator Notes:

---

---

# Investment Committee Summary Page

Summarize material deal facts, risks, and projected outcomes for decision review.
Provide objective analysis without advocacy language.

## DEAL IDENTIFICATION

Property Name / Address:

___

Asset Type:

___

Submarket:

___

Acquisition Structure:

___

## TRANSACTION SUMMARY

Proposed Purchase Price:

___

Estimated All-In Capital Requirement:

___

Equity Required:

___

Financing Structure:

___

Projected Stabilized NOI:

___

Projected Exit Value:

___

Projected Equity Multiple:

___

Projected IRR (if applicable):

___

## CAPITAL STACK OVERVIEW

Total Senior Debt:

___

Subordinate / Mezz Debt:

___

Equity Contribution %:

___

DSCR at Stabilization:

___

Liquidity Stability Level:

- □ Strong
- □ Moderate

- □ Fragile

**VALUE CREATION STRATEGY**

Primary Value Drivers:

___

Operational Improvements:

___

Capital Improvements:

___

Timeline to Stabilization:

___

**RISK SUMMARY**

Top 3 Identified Risks:

___

___

___

Primary Risk Category:

- □ Financial
- □ Legal
- □ Capital Stack
- □ Market
- □ Operational
- □ Liquidity
- □ Other

Stress Test Outcome:

- □ Stable Under Stress
- □ Marginal Under Stress
- □ Breaks Under Stress

**EXIT STRATEGY SUMMARY**

Primary Exit Strategy:

___

Target Hold Period:

___

Sensitivity to Cap Rate Expansion:

___

Liquidity at Exit (Projected):

___

**RECOMMENDATION**

Recommendation:

- □ Proceed
- □ Proceed with Modifications
- □ Defer
- □ Reject

Phase II
FeasibiltyConditions Required to Proceed:

Conditions Required to Proceed:

______________________________________________

______________________________________________

Approval Authority Signature (Optional Discipline Mechanism):

______________________________________________

Date:

______________________________________________

# Deal Kill Criteria Checklist

Identify predefined conditions that require termination of pursuit.
Apply criteria objectively without regard to sunk cost.

**ECONOMIC KILL CRITERIA**

□ Senior Position Fully Covered by Verified Value
□ Implied Equity Positive After Conservative Valuation
□ Short Sale Recovery Inferior to Foreclosure
□ IRR Below Minimum Threshold
□ Equity Multiple Below Target
□ Liquidity Insufficient for Stabilization
□ Repair Budget Exceeds Acceptable Variance
□ Cap Rate Expansion Eliminates Return
□ Stress Scenario Breaks Capital Stack

Details (if triggered):

---

**CAPITAL STRUCTURE KILL CRITERIA**

□ Financing Commitment Not Obtainable
□ Equity Commitments Soft / Unverified
□ Lender Requires Excessive Cash Contribution
□ Unacceptable Recourse Exposure
□ Personal Guarantee Risk Outside Tolerance
□ Intercreditor Structure Blocks Resolution
□ Junior Lienholder Refuses Economic Settlement

Details:

---

**LEGAL / TITLE KILL CRITERIA**

□ Uninsurable Title Condition
□ Unresolved Environmental Liability
□ Pending Litigation Creates Material Risk
□ Bankruptcy Complication Not Resolvable
□ Cross-Collateralization Exposure Too Broad
□ Regulatory or Zoning Impairment

Details:

---

**OPERATIONAL KILL CRITERIA**

□ Structural Deficiency Beyond Budget
□ Major Tenant Departure Imminent
□ Market Liquidity Insufficient
□ Lease-Up Risk Excessive
□ Insurance Coverage Unavailable or Cost Prohibitive

Details:

---

## SPONSOR / BEHAVIORAL KILL CRITERIA

- □ Borrower Cooperation Collapses
- □ Hidden Stakeholder Veto Identified
- □ Material Misrepresentation Discovered
- □ Documentation Withheld
- □ Communication Breakdown with Lender

Details:

---

## FINAL REVIEW

Any Kill Criteria Triggered?

- □ Yes
- □ No

If Yes — Terminate Pursuit?

- □ Yes
- □ No
- □ Conditional Review

Decision Rationale:

________________________________________

________________________________________

Reviewed By:

________________________________________

Date:

________________________________________

# Investor Strategy Notes

Document strategic observations, negotiation posture, and capital positioning considerations. Use this section for structured thinking prior to submission and during feasibility reassessment.

**STRATEGIC THESIS**

Investment Rationale (Core Thesis):

Why This Asset is Mispriced:

**LENDER POSITIONING STRATEGY**

Primary Argument to Senior Lender:

Anticipated Objections:

Negotiation Leverage Points:

**JUNIOR / SUBORDINATE STRATEGY**

Settlement Approach:

Timing Strategy:

Risk of Holdout Behavior:

**CAPITAL POSITIONING STRATEGY**

Equity Narrative to Investors:

Return Justification Under Stress:

Liquidity Cushion Philosophy:

## MARKET STRATEGY

Submarket Dynamics Observed:

______________________________________________________________________

______________________________________________________________________

Competitive Supply Threat:

______________________________________________________________________

Exit Liquidity Observations:

______________________________________________________________________

## TIMELINE STRATEGY

Clock Advantage / Disadvantage:

______________________________________________________________________

Optimal Submission Window:

______________________________________________________________________

Acceleration Risk Awareness:

______________________________________________________________________

## RISK MITIGATION STRATEGY

Top Strategic Risk:

______________________________________________________________________

Mitigation Plan:

______________________________________________________________________

______________________________________________________________________

Fallback Strategy if Feasibility Weakens:

______________________________________________________________________

## OPERATOR REFLECTION

Is Conviction Based on Data or Emotion?

______________________________________________________________________

What Would Cause Immediate Withdrawal?

______________________________________________________________________

Does This Align With Portfolio Objectives?

______________________________________________________________________

# Investor Strategy Notes

Document strategic observations, negotiation posture, and capital positioning considerations. Use this section for structured thinking prior to submission and during feasibility reassessment.

**STRATEGIC THESIS**

Investment Rationale (Core Thesis):

______________________________________________

______________________________________________

______________________________________________

______________________________________________

Why This Asset is Mispriced:

______________________________________________

______________________________________________

______________________________________________

**LENDER POSITIONING STRATEGY**

Primary Argument to Senior Lender:

______________________________________________

______________________________________________

Anticipated Objections:

______________________________________________

______________________________________________

Negotiation Leverage Points:

______________________________________________

______________________________________________

**JUNIOR / SUBORDINATE STRATEGY**

Settlement Approach:

______________________________________________

______________________________________________

Timing Strategy:

______________________________________________

Risk of Holdout Behavior:

______________________________________________

**CAPITAL POSITIONING STRATEGY**

Equity Narrative to Investors:

______________________________________________

______________________________________________

Return Justification Under Stress:

______________________________________________

Liquidity Cushion Philosophy:

______________________________________________

**MARKET STRATEGY**

Submarket Dynamics Observed:

_______________________________________________

_______________________________________________

Competitive Supply Threat:

_______________________________________________

Exit Liquidity Observations:

_______________________________________________

**TIMELINE STRATEGY**

Clock Advantage / Disadvantage:

_______________________________________________

Optimal Submission Window:

_______________________________________________

Acceleration Risk Awareness:

_______________________________________________

**RISK MITIGATION STRATEGY**

Top Strategic Risk:

_______________________________________________

Mitigation Plan:

_______________________________________________

_______________________________________________

Fallback Strategy if Feasibility Weakens:

_______________________________________________

**OPERATOR REFLECTION**

Is Conviction Based on Data or Emotion?

_______________________________________________

What Would Cause Immediate Withdrawal?

_______________________________________________

Does This Align With Portfolio Objectives?

_______________________________________________

# Investor Strategy Notes

Document strategic observations, negotiation posture, and capital positioning considerations. Use this section for structured thinking prior to submission and during feasibility reassessment.

**STRATEGIC THESIS**

Investment Rationale (Core Thesis):

Why This Asset is Mispriced:

**LENDER POSITIONING STRATEGY**

Primary Argument to Senior Lender:

Anticipated Objections:

Negotiation Leverage Points:

**JUNIOR / SUBORDINATE STRATEGY**

Settlement Approach:

Timing Strategy:

Risk of Holdout Behavior:

**CAPITAL POSITIONING STRATEGY**

Equity Narrative to Investors:

Return Justification Under Stress:

Liquidity Cushion Philosophy:

## MARKET STRATEGY

Submarket Dynamics Observed:

Competitive Supply Threat:

Exit Liquidity Observations:

## TIMELINE STRATEGY

Clock Advantage / Disadvantage:

Optimal Submission Window:

Acceleration Risk Awareness:

## RISK MITIGATION STRATEGY

Top Strategic Risk:

Mitigation Plan:

Fallback Strategy if Feasibility Weakens:

## OPERATOR REFLECTION

Is Conviction Based on Data or Emotion?

What Would Cause Immediate Withdrawal?

Does This Align With Portfolio Objectives?

# Investor Strategy Notes

Document strategic observations, negotiation posture, and capital positioning considerations. Use this section for structured thinking prior to submission and during feasibility reassessment.

**STRATEGIC THESIS**

Investment Rationale (Core Thesis):

Why This Asset is Mispriced:

**LENDER POSITIONING STRATEGY**

Primary Argument to Senior Lender:

Anticipated Objections:

Negotiation Leverage Points:

**JUNIOR / SUBORDINATE STRATEGY**

Settlement Approach:

Timing Strategy:

Risk of Holdout Behavior:

**CAPITAL POSITIONING STRATEGY**

Equity Narrative to Investors:

Return Justification Under Stress:

Liquidity Cushion Philosophy:

## MARKET STRATEGY

Submarket Dynamics Observed:

Competitive Supply Threat:

Exit Liquidity Observations:

## TIMELINE STRATEGY

Clock Advantage / Disadvantage:

Optimal Submission Window:

Acceleration Risk Awareness:

## RISK MITIGATION STRATEGY

Top Strategic Risk:

Mitigation Plan:

Fallback Strategy if Feasibility Weakens:

## OPERATOR REFLECTION

Is Conviction Based on Data or Emotion?

What Would Cause Immediate Withdrawal?

Does This Align With Portfolio Objectives?

# Investor Strategy Notes

Document strategic observations, negotiation posture, and capital positioning considerations. Use this section for structured thinking prior to submission and during feasibility reassessment.

**STRATEGIC THESIS**

Investment Rationale (Core Thesis):

Why This Asset is Mispriced:

**LENDER POSITIONING STRATEGY**

Primary Argument to Senior Lender:

Anticipated Objections:

Negotiation Leverage Points:

**JUNIOR / SUBORDINATE STRATEGY**

Settlement Approach:

Timing Strategy:

Risk of Holdout Behavior:

**CAPITAL POSITIONING STRATEGY**

Equity Narrative to Investors:

Return Justification Under Stress:

Liquidity Cushion Philosophy:

**MARKET STRATEGY**

Submarket Dynamics Observed:

____________________________________________________________

____________________________________________________________

Competitive Supply Threat:

____________________________________________________________

Exit Liquidity Observations:

____________________________________________________________

**TIMELINE STRATEGY**

Clock Advantage / Disadvantage:

____________________________________________________________

Optimal Submission Window:

____________________________________________________________

Acceleration Risk Awareness:

____________________________________________________________

**RISK MITIGATION STRATEGY**

Top Strategic Risk:

____________________________________________________________

Mitigation Plan:

____________________________________________________________

____________________________________________________________

Fallback Strategy if Feasibility Weakens:

____________________________________________________________

**OPERATOR REFLECTION**

Is Conviction Based on Data or Emotion?

____________________________________________________________

What Would Cause Immediate Withdrawal?

____________________________________________________________

Does This Align With Portfolio Objectives?

____________________________________________________________

# Investor Strategy Notes

Document strategic observations, negotiation posture, and capital positioning considerations. Use this section for structured thinking prior to submission and during feasibility reassessment.

**STRATEGIC THESIS**

Investment Rationale (Core Thesis):

Why This Asset is Mispriced:

**LENDER POSITIONING STRATEGY**

Primary Argument to Senior Lender:

Anticipated Objections:

Negotiation Leverage Points:

**JUNIOR / SUBORDINATE STRATEGY**

Settlement Approach:

Timing Strategy:

Risk of Holdout Behavior:

**CAPITAL POSITIONING STRATEGY**

Equity Narrative to Investors:

Return Justification Under Stress:

Liquidity Cushion Philosophy:

## MARKET STRATEGY

Submarket Dynamics Observed:

Competitive Supply Threat:

Exit Liquidity Observations:

## TIMELINE STRATEGY

Clock Advantage / Disadvantage:

Optimal Submission Window:

Acceleration Risk Awareness:

## RISK MITIGATION STRATEGY

Top Strategic Risk:

Mitigation Plan:

Fallback Strategy if Feasibility Weakens:

## OPERATOR REFLECTION

Is Conviction Based on Data or Emotion?

What Would Cause Immediate Withdrawal?

Does This Align With Portfolio Objectives?

# Gate II – Feasibility Authorization

## ADVANCEMENT AUTHORIZATION

Advancement to Phase III — Structuring is authorized only when feasibility analysis supports a defensible net position, acceptable risk exposure, and alignment with predefined kill criteria.

If material deficiencies or risk concentrations exist, they must be documented prior to advancement.

## FEASIBILITY CONFIRMATION

Confirm the following:

- □ Equity Position Analysis Completed
- □ Market Value Estimation Supported by Comparable Data
- □ Repair & Deferred Maintenance Accurately Estimated
- □ Net-to-Lender Feasibility Model Supports Viability
- □ Capital Stack Requirements Confirmed
- □ Cash Requirement & Liquidity Adequate
- □ Exit Strategy Defined
- □ Scenario Stress Test Performed
- □ Kill Criteria Reviewed and Not Triggered

## RISK THRESHOLD REVIEW

Are Risk Flags Within Acceptable Threshold?

- □ Yes
- □ No

Does Return Profile Justify Identified Risk?

- □ Yes
- □ No

Is Timeline Exposure Acceptable?

- □ Yes
- □ No

Is Capital at Risk Within Predefined Limits?

- □ Yes
- □ No

## DEFICIENCIES / CONDITIONAL ADVANCEMENT NOTES

If advancement is conditional, document specific deficiencies and mitigation requirements.

______________________________________________

______________________________________________

______________________________________________

______________________________________________

## ADVANCEMENT STATUS

- □ Authorized — Advance to Phase III
- □ Authorized with Conditions
- □ Defer Advancement
- □ Do Not Advance

If Defer or Do Not Advance, document rationale:

---

---

**AUTHORIZED SIGNATORY**

Name: ______________________________

Title / Role: _________________________

Signature: ___________________________

Date: _______________________________

Authority Basis (if applicable):

- □ Sole Operator
- □ Managing Member
- □ General Partner
- □ Investment Committee
- □ Other

## Phase II — Structured Notes

Document observations, tactical considerations, or material developments not captured in structured worksheets.
Maintain objective, execution-focused notation.

# PHASE III
# STRUCTURING

(Loss Mitigation & Transaction Control Path)

# Orientation

**Phase III defines negotiation posture and structural strategy.**

This phase establishes:

- Offer structure
- Concession boundaries
- Junior lien approach
- Capital alignment
- Escalation framework
- Timeline positioning

Structuring translates feasibility into executable strategy.

Advancement beyond this phase requires clarity regarding position, leverage, and defined limits.

***"Structure Precedes Leverage."***

# Hardship Narrative Development Worksheet

Develop a structured hardship narrative consistent with documented financial and operational conditions. Avoid emotional framing or unsupported claims.

### HARDSHIP CATEGORY IDENTIFICATION

Primary Hardship Type:

- □ Income Reduction
- □ Business Failure
- □ Market Decline
- □ Tenant Loss
- □ Medical Event
- □ Divorce / Separation
- □ Death of Key Party
- □ Interest Rate Reset
- □ Balloon Maturity
- □ Operational Mismanagement
- □ Other

Secondary Contributing Factors:

______________________________________________

______________________________________________

### TIMELINE OF DISTRESS

Date Hardship Began:

______________________________________________

Date of First Missed Payment:

______________________________________________

Attempts to Cure Default:

______________________________________________

______________________________________________

Forbearance / Modification Discussions:

______________________________________________

### FINANCIAL IMPACT SUMMARY

Monthly Income Before Hardship:

______________________________________________

Current Monthly Income:

______________________________________________

Monthly Debt Service Obligation:

______________________________________________

Monthly Operating Deficit (if applicable):

______________________________________________

Liquidity Remaining:

______________________________________________

Is Recovery Realistic Without Resolution?

- □ Yes

Phase III
Structuring□ No

□ No
□ Unlikely

**PROPERTY PERFORMANCE FACTORS**

Vacancy Increase (if applicable):

______________________________

Expense Increases:

______________________________

Market Decline Evidence:

______________________________

Deferred Maintenance Impact:

______________________________

**GOOD FAITH INDICATORS**

Has Borrower Attempted to Market Property?
□ Yes
□ No
Has Borrower Contributed Cash During Distress?
□ Yes
□ No
Has Borrower Provided Full Documentation?
□ Yes
□ No
Is Borrower Cooperative?
□ Yes
□ No
□ Inconsistent

**DEFICIENCY POSITION AWARENESS**

Does Borrower Acknowledge Deficiency Exposure?
□ Yes
□ No
Is Borrower Requesting Full Release?
□ Yes
□ No
Is Partial Contribution Proposed?

______________________________

**DRAFT NARRATIVE OUTLINE**

Opening Context (1–2 Sentences):

______________________________

______________________________

Description of Hardship:

______________________________

Financial Impact Summary:

Resolution Request Framing:

**NARRATIVE RISK REVIEW**

Does Narrative Align With Financial Statement?

- □ Yes
- □ No

Any Inconsistencies Identified?

Is Narrative Likely to Withstand Lender Scrutiny?

- □ Yes
- □ No

# Borrower Financial Statement Audit

Review borrower financial disclosures for completeness, consistency, and alignment with hardship narrative. Identify discrepancies prior to submission.

**DOCUMENTATION RECEIVED**

Personal Financial Statement Provided?

- □ Yes
- □ No

Business Financial Statement Provided?

- □ Yes
- □ No

Bank Statements (Last 2–3 Months):

- □ Complete
- □ Partial
- □ Not Provided

Tax Returns Provided (Most Recent 2 Years):

- □ Yes
- □ No

Profit & Loss Statement Provided?

- □ Yes
- □ No

Rent Roll Provided (if applicable)?

- □ Yes
- □ No

**INCOME VERIFICATION**

Gross Monthly Income (Stated):

______________________________________________

Gross Monthly Income (Verified from Docs):

______________________________________________

Variance Identified?

- □ Yes
- □ No

Source of Income Verified?

- □ Yes
- □ No

Unreported Income Suspected?

- □ Yes
- □ No
- □ Unknown

Notes:

______________________________________________

**EXPENSE ANALYSIS**

Total Monthly Expenses (Stated):

Total Monthly Expenses (Calculated from Docs):

Debt Obligations (Non-Subject):

Are Expenses Inflated or Understated?

- □ Inflated
- □ Understated
- □ Consistent

Material Discrepancies Identified?

**ASSET REVIEW**

Cash on Hand (Declared):

Cash Verified via Bank Statements:

Retirement Accounts Identified:

Real Estate Holdings Outside Subject:

Business Ownership Interests:

Liquid Assets Available for Contribution?

- □ Yes
- □ No
- □ Uncertain

**LIABILITY REVIEW**

Total Liabilities (Declared):

Additional Liabilities Identified:

Pending Judgments / Lawsuits:

Tax Liabilities:

Contingent Liabilities:

**DEFICIENCY CAPACITY ANALYSIS**

Does Borrower Have Capacity to Contribute?

- □ Yes
- □ No
- □ Limited

Estimated Reasonable Contribution (if any):

---

Is Borrower Financially Insolvent?

- □ Yes
- □ No
- □ Marginal

Would Lender Likely Demand Contribution?

- □ Yes
- □ No
- □ Possible

## CONSISTENCY CHECK

Does Hardship Narrative Align With Financial Data?

- □ Yes
- □ No

Are There Inconsistencies That Require Explanation?

- □ Yes
- □ No

If Yes, Describe:

______________________________

______________________________

## AUDIT CONCLUSION

Financial Disclosure Integrity Level:

- □ Strong
- □ Moderate
- □ Weak

Submission Ready?

- □ Yes
- □ Requires Correction
- □ Incomplete

Reviewed By:

______________________________

Date:

______________________________

# Document Submission Checklist

Confirm completeness and accuracy of all required documentation prior to submission.
Re-verify time-sensitive documents before resubmission.

**BORROWER DOCUMENTATION**

□ Hardship Letter
□ Borrower Financial Statement
□ Personal Financial Statement
□ Business Financial Statement
□ Bank Statements (Last 2–3 Months)
□ Most Recent Tax Returns (2 Years)
□ Profit & Loss Statement (YTD)
□ Rent Roll (If Applicable)
□ Lease Agreements (If Requested)
□ Corporate Resolution / Authority Documentation
□ Operating Agreement / Entity Documents
□ ID Verification (If Required)

Missing or Incomplete Items:

---

**PROPERTY DOCUMENTATION**

□ Purchase Contract (Executed)
□ Proof of Funds
□ Preliminary Settlement Statement (HUD / Net Sheet)
□ Title Commitment
□ Property Condition Report (If Available)
□ Environmental Report (If Available)
□ Insurance Declaration Page
□ Property Tax Statements
□ Utility Statements (If Requested)

Deficiencies Identified:

---

**OFFER PACKAGE COMPONENTS**

□ Short Sale Authorization Form
□ Listing Agreement (If Required)
□ Marketing History Documentation
□ Comparable Sales Package
□ Repair Estimates
□ Net-to-Lender Analysis
□ Buyer Qualification Letter
□ Earnest Money Proof
□ Lender-Specific Forms Completed

Are All Lender-Specific Forms Current Version?

□ Yes
□ No

## TIME-SENSITIVE DOCUMENT CHECK

Bank Statements Dated Within 30–60 Days?

□ Yes

□ No

Tax Returns Most Recent Filed Year?

□ Yes

□ No

Financial Statements Signed & Dated?

□ Yes

□ No

Hardship Letter Dated Within 30 Days?

□ Yes

□ No

Are Any Documents Stale?

□ Yes

□ No

## SUBMISSION FORMAT REVIEW

Submission Method:

□ Portal Upload

□ Email

□ Physical Mail

□ Other

File Naming Convention Consistent?

□ Yes

□ No

PDF Combined and Ordered Properly?

□ Yes

□ No

Confirmation of Receipt Obtained?

□ Yes

□ No

Date Submitted:

______________________________________________

## DEFICIENCY TRACKING

Deficiency Notice Received?

□ Yes

□ No

Date of Deficiency Notice:

______________________________________________

Items Requested by Lender:

______________________________________________

______________________________________________

Date Resubmitted:

## CONTROL VERIFICATION

Is Package Complete and Internally Verified?

- □ Yes
- □ No

Second-Level Review Completed?

- □ Yes
- □ No

Reviewed By:

______________________________

Date:

______________________________

# Submission Record Log

Record each document submission, resubmission, and lender request.
Maintain chronological accuracy and retain confirmation evidence.

**SUBMISSION LOG TABLE**

| Date Submitted | Submission Type | Documents Included | Method | Confirm Received | Lender Contact | Notes |
|---|---|---|---|---|---|---|
| | | | | | | |
| | | | | | | |
| | | | | | | |
| | | | | | | |
| | | | | | | |
| | | | | | | |
| | | | | | | |
| | | | | | | |
| | | | | | | |
| | | | | | | |

| Date Submitted | Submission Type | Documents Included | Method | Confirm Received | Lender Contact | Notes |
|---|---|---|---|---|---|---|
| | | | | | | |
| | | | | | | |

**Date Submitted**

→ Exact calendar date

**Submission Type**

→ Initial Package / Partial Upload / Deficiency Response / Update / Revised Net Sheet / Etc.

**Documents Included**

→ Short summary (e.g., "Full Package + Updated Financials")

**Method**

→ Portal / Email / Physical Mail / Secure Link

**Confirmation Received**

→ Yes / No / Tracking # / Email Confirmation

**Lender Contact**

→ Asset Manager / Processor / Portal Case ID

**Notes**

→ Brief clarification

## DEFICIENCY RESPONSE TRACKING

| Date Requested | Items Requested | Date Responded | Outstanding? |
|---|---|---|---|
| | | | |
| | | | |
| | | | |
| | | | |
| | | | |
| | | | |
| | | | |

Phase III
Structuring

| | | | |
|---|---|---|---|
| | | | |

**CONTROL CONFIRMATION**

Is Most Recent Submission Confirmed Received?

- □ Yes
- □ No

Any Documents Pending Confirmation?

- □ Yes
- □ No

Date of Last Confirmed Receipt:

___

# Submission Record Log

Record each document submission, resubmission, and lender request.
Maintain chronological accuracy and retain confirmation evidence.

**SUBMISSION LOG TABLE**

| Date Submitted | Submission Type | Documents Included | Method | Confirm Received | Lender Contact | Notes |
|---|---|---|---|---|---|---|
| | | | | | | |
| | | | | | | |
| | | | | | | |
| | | | | | | |
| | | | | | | |
| | | | | | | |
| | | | | | | |
| | | | | | | |
| | | | | | | |
| | | | | | | |

Phase III
Structuring

| Date Submitted | Submission Type | Documents Included | Method | Confirm Received | Lender Contact | Notes |
|---|---|---|---|---|---|---|
| | | | | | | |
| | | | | | | |

**Date Submitted**

→ Exact calendar date

**Submission Type**

→ Initial Package / Partial Upload / Deficiency Response / Update / Revised Net Sheet / Etc.

**Documents Included**

→ Short summary (e.g., "Full Package + Updated Financials")

**Method**

→ Portal / Email / Physical Mail / Secure Link

**Confirmation Received**

→ Yes / No / Tracking # / Email Confirmation

**Lender Contact**

→ Asset Manager / Processor / Portal Case ID

**Notes**

→ Brief clarification

## DEFICIENCY RESPONSE TRACKING

| Date Requested | Items Requested | Date Responded | Outstanding? |
|---|---|---|---|
| | | | |
| | | | |
| | | | |
| | | | |
| | | | |
| | | | |
| | | | |

| | | | |
|---|---|---|---|
| | | | |

## CONTROL CONFIRMATION

Is Most Recent Submission Confirmed Received?

- □ Yes
- □ No

Any Documents Pending Confirmation?

- □ Yes
- □ No

Date of Last Confirmed Receipt:

---

# Submission Record Log

Record each document submission, resubmission, and lender request.
Maintain chronological accuracy and retain confirmation evidence.

## SUBMISSION LOG TABLE

| Date Submitted | Submission Type | Documents Included | Method | Confirm Received | Lender Contact | Notes |
|---|---|---|---|---|---|---|
| | | | | | | |
| | | | | | | |
| | | | | | | |
| | | | | | | |
| | | | | | | |
| | | | | | | |
| | | | | | | |
| | | | | | | |
| | | | | | | |
| | | | | | | |

| Date Submitted | Submission Type | Documents Included | Method | Confirm Received | Lender Contact | Notes |
|---|---|---|---|---|---|---|
| | | | | | | |
| | | | | | | |

**Date Submitted**

→ Exact calendar date

**Submission Type**

→ Initial Package / Partial Upload / Deficiency Response / Update / Revised Net Sheet / Etc.

**Documents Included**

→ Short summary (e.g., "Full Package + Updated Financials")

**Method**

→ Portal / Email / Physical Mail / Secure Link

**Confirmation Received**

→ Yes / No / Tracking # / Email Confirmation

**Lender Contact**

→ Asset Manager / Processor / Portal Case ID

**Notes**

→ Brief clarification

## DEFICIENCY RESPONSE TRACKING

| Date Requested | Items Requested | Date Responded | Outstanding? |
|---|---|---|---|
| | | | |
| | | | |
| | | | |
| | | | |
| | | | |
| | | | |
| | | | |

Phase III
Structuring

| | | | |
|---|---|---|---|
| | | | |

## CONTROL CONFIRMATION

Is Most Recent Submission Confirmed Received?

- □ Yes
- □ No

Any Documents Pending Confirmation?

- □ Yes
- □ No

Date of Last Confirmed Receipt:

______________________________

# Submission Record Log

Record each document submission, resubmission, and lender request.
Maintain chronological accuracy and retain confirmation evidence.

**SUBMISSION LOG TABLE**

| Date Submitted | Submission Type | Documents Included | Method | Confirm Received | Lender Contact | Notes |
|---|---|---|---|---|---|---|
| | | | | | | |
| | | | | | | |
| | | | | | | |
| | | | | | | |
| | | | | | | |
| | | | | | | |
| | | | | | | |
| | | | | | | |
| | | | | | | |
| | | | | | | |

Phase III
Structuring

| Date Submitted | Submission Type | Documents Included | Method | Confirm Received | Lender Contact | Notes |
|---|---|---|---|---|---|---|
| | | | | | | |
| | | | | | | |

**Date Submitted**

→ Exact calendar date

**Submission Type**

→ Initial Package / Partial Upload / Deficiency Response / Update / Revised Net Sheet / Etc.

**Documents Included**

→ Short summary (e.g., "Full Package + Updated Financials")

**Method**

→ Portal / Email / Physical Mail / Secure Link

**Confirmation Received**

→ Yes / No / Tracking # / Email Confirmation

**Lender Contact**

→ Asset Manager / Processor / Portal Case ID

**Notes**

→ Brief clarification

**DEFICIENCY RESPONSE TRACKING**

| Date Requested | Items Requested | Date Responded | Outstanding? |
|---|---|---|---|
| | | | |
| | | | |
| | | | |
| | | | |
| | | | |
| | | | |
| | | | |

| | | | |
|---|---|---|---|
| | | | |

**CONTROL CONFIRMATION**

Is Most Recent Submission Confirmed Received?

- □ Yes
- □ No

Any Documents Pending Confirmation?

- □ Yes
- □ No

Date of Last Confirmed Receipt:

---

# Submission Record Log

Record each document submission, resubmission, and lender request.
Maintain chronological accuracy and retain confirmation evidence.

**SUBMISSION LOG TABLE**

| Date Submitted | Submission Type | Documents Included | Method | Confirm Received | Lender Contact | Notes |
|---|---|---|---|---|---|---|
| | | | | | | |
| | | | | | | |
| | | | | | | |
| | | | | | | |
| | | | | | | |
| | | | | | | |
| | | | | | | |
| | | | | | | |
| | | | | | | |
| | | | | | | |

| Date Submitted | Submission Type | Documents Included | Method | Confirm Received | Lender Contact | Notes |
|---|---|---|---|---|---|---|
| | | | | | | |
| | | | | | | |

**Date Submitted**

→ Exact calendar date

**Submission Type**

→ Initial Package / Partial Upload / Deficiency Response / Update / Revised Net Sheet / Etc.

**Documents Included**

→ Short summary (e.g., "Full Package + Updated Financials")

**Method**

→ Portal / Email / Physical Mail / Secure Link

**Confirmation Received**

→ Yes / No / Tracking # / Email Confirmation

**Lender Contact**

→ Asset Manager / Processor / Portal Case ID

**Notes**

→ Brief clarification

## DEFICIENCY RESPONSE TRACKING

| Date Requested | Items Requested | Date Responded | Outstanding? |
|---|---|---|---|
| | | | |
| | | | |
| | | | |
| | | | |
| | | | |
| | | | |
| | | | |

Phase III
Structuring

| | | | |
|---|---|---|---|
| | | | |

**CONTROL CONFIRMATION**

Is Most Recent Submission Confirmed Received?

- □ Yes
- □ No

Any Documents Pending Confirmation?

- □ Yes
- □ No

Date of Last Confirmed Receipt:

______________________________________________

# Submission Record Log

Record each document submission, resubmission, and lender request.
Maintain chronological accuracy and retain confirmation evidence.

**SUBMISSION LOG TABLE**

| Date Submitted | Submission Type | Documents Included | Method | Confirm Received | Lender Contact | Notes |
|---|---|---|---|---|---|---|
| | | | | | | |
| | | | | | | |
| | | | | | | |
| | | | | | | |
| | | | | | | |
| | | | | | | |
| | | | | | | |
| | | | | | | |
| | | | | | | |
| | | | | | | |

Phase III
Structuring

| Date Submitted | Submission Type | Documents Included | Method | Confirm Received | Lender Contact | Notes |
|---|---|---|---|---|---|---|
| | | | | | | |
| | | | | | | |

**Date Submitted**

→ Exact calendar date

**Submission Type**

→ Initial Package / Partial Upload / Deficiency Response / Update / Revised Net Sheet / Etc.

**Documents Included**

→ Short summary (e.g., "Full Package + Updated Financials")

**Method**

→ Portal / Email / Physical Mail / Secure Link

**Confirmation Received**

→ Yes / No / Tracking # / Email Confirmation

**Lender Contact**

→ Asset Manager / Processor / Portal Case ID

**Notes**

→ Brief clarification

**DEFICIENCY RESPONSE TRACKING**

| Date Requested | Items Requested | Date Responded | Outstanding? |
|---|---|---|---|
| | | | |
| | | | |
| | | | |
| | | | |
| | | | |
| | | | |
| | | | |

| | | | |
|---|---|---|---|
| | | | |

**CONTROL CONFIRMATION**

Is Most Recent Submission Confirmed Received?

- □ Yes
- □ No

Any Documents Pending Confirmation?

- □ Yes
- □ No

Date of Last Confirmed Receipt:

# Lender Communication Log

Document all material communication with lender representatives.

Record factual content only. Avoid interpretation or opinion.

---

## COMMUNICATION LOG TABLE

| Date | Contact Name | Title / Role | Method | Summary of Discussion | Commitments Made | Follow-Up Required | Next Action Date |
|---|---|---|---|---|---|---|---|
| | | | | | | | |
| | | | | | | | |
| | | | | | | | |
| | | | | | | | |
| | | | | | | | |
| | | | | | | | |
| | | | | | | | |
| | | | | | | | |
| | | | | | | | |
| | | | | | | | |
| | | | | | | | |
| | | | | | | | |

**Column Definitions**

**Date**

→ Calendar date

**Contact Name**

→ Asset Manager / Processor / Supervisor

**Title / Role**

→ Asset Manager / Special Assets / Workout Officer / Etc.

**Method**

→ Phone / Email / Portal Message / In Person

**Summary of Discussion**

→ Objective summary only

**Commitments Made**

→ What lender agreed to (if anything)

**Follow-Up Required**

→ What operator must provide

**Next Action Date**

→ Deadline for next touchpoint

**ESCALATION NOTE SECTION**

Escalation Trigger Identified:

________________________________________

________________________________________

________________________________________

________________________________________

Supervisor Contact Initiated?

□ Yes
□ No

Date of Escalation:

________________________________________

**COMMUNICATION PATTERN REVIEW**

Response Time Trend:

□ Prompt
□ Moderate Delay
□ Slow / Non-Responsive

Communication Tone Observed:

□ Cooperative
□ Neutral
□ Defensive
□ Adversarial

Is Relationship Improving?

□ Yes
□ No
□ Stalled

**CONTROL CONFIRMATION**

Last Confirmed File Status:

________________________________________

Next Required Submission Date:

________________________________________

Operator Initials:

________________________________________

Phase III
StructuringDate:

Date:

---

# Lender Communication Log

Document all material communication with lender representatives.
Record factual content only. Avoid interpretation or opinion.

---

## COMMUNICATION LOG TABLE

| Date | Contact Name | Title / Role | Method | Summary of Discussion | Commitments Made | Follow-Up Required | Next Action Date |
|---|---|---|---|---|---|---|---|
| | | | | | | | |
| | | | | | | | |
| | | | | | | | |
| | | | | | | | |
| | | | | | | | |
| | | | | | | | |
| | | | | | | | |
| | | | | | | | |
| | | | | | | | |
| | | | | | | | |
| | | | | | | | |
| | | | | | | | |

**Column Definitions**

**Date**

→ Calendar date

**Contact Name**

→ Asset Manager / Processor / Supervisor

**Title / Role**

Phase III
Structuring→ Asset Manager / Special Assets / Workout Officer / Etc.

→ Asset Manager / Special Assets / Workout Officer / Etc.

**Method**

→ Phone / Email / Portal Message / In Person

**Summary of Discussion**

→ Objective summary only

**Commitments Made**

→ What lender agreed to (if anything)

**Follow-Up Required**

→ What operator must provide

**Next Action Date**

→ Deadline for next touchpoint

**ESCALATION NOTE SECTION**

Escalation Trigger Identified:

___

___

___

___

Supervisor Contact Initiated?

□ Yes
□ No

Date of Escalation:

___

**COMMUNICATION PATTERN REVIEW**

Response Time Trend:

□ Prompt
□ Moderate Delay
□ Slow / Non-Responsive

Communication Tone Observed:

□ Cooperative
□ Neutral
□ Defensive
□ Adversarial

Is Relationship Improving?

□ Yes
□ No
□ Stalled

**CONTROL CONFIRMATION**

Last Confirmed File Status:

___

Next Required Submission Date:

___

Operator Initials:

___

Date:

# Lender Communication Log

Document all material communication with lender representatives.

Record factual content only. Avoid interpretation or opinion.

---

## COMMUNICATION LOG TABLE

| Date | Contact Name | Title / Role | Method | Summary of Discussion | Commitments Made | Follow-Up Required | Next Action Date |
|---|---|---|---|---|---|---|---|
| | | | | | | | |
| | | | | | | | |
| | | | | | | | |
| | | | | | | | |
| | | | | | | | |
| | | | | | | | |
| | | | | | | | |
| | | | | | | | |
| | | | | | | | |
| | | | | | | | |
| | | | | | | | |
| | | | | | | | |

**Column Definitions**

**Date**

→ Calendar date

**Contact Name**

→ Asset Manager / Processor / Supervisor

**Title / Role**
→ Asset Manager / Special Assets / Workout Officer / Etc.
**Method**
→ Phone / Email / Portal Message / In Person
**Summary of Discussion**
→ Objective summary only
**Commitments Made**
→ What lender agreed to (if anything)
**Follow-Up Required**
→ What operator must provide
**Next Action Date**
→ Deadline for next touchpoint

## ESCALATION NOTE SECTION

Escalation Trigger Identified:

______________________________________________

______________________________________________

______________________________________________

______________________________________________

Supervisor Contact Initiated?
□ Yes
□ No

Date of Escalation:

______________________________________________

## COMMUNICATION PATTERN REVIEW

Response Time Trend:
□ Prompt
□ Moderate Delay
□ Slow / Non-Responsive

Communication Tone Observed:
□ Cooperative
□ Neutral
□ Defensive
□ Adversarial

Is Relationship Improving?
□ Yes
□ No
□ Stalled

## CONTROL CONFIRMATION

Last Confirmed File Status:

______________________________________________

Next Required Submission Date:

______________________________________________

Operator Initials:

______________________________________________

Phase III
StructuringDate:

Date:

---

# Lender Communication Log

Document all material communication with lender representatives.
Record factual content only. Avoid interpretation or opinion.

---

### COMMUNICATION LOG TABLE

| Date | Contact Name | Title / Role | Method | Summary of Discussion | Commitments Made | Follow-Up Required | Next Action Date |
|---|---|---|---|---|---|---|---|
| | | | | | | | |
| | | | | | | | |
| | | | | | | | |
| | | | | | | | |
| | | | | | | | |
| | | | | | | | |
| | | | | | | | |
| | | | | | | | |
| | | | | | | | |
| | | | | | | | |
| | | | | | | | |
| | | | | | | | |

**Column Definitions**

**Date**

→ Calendar date

**Contact Name**

→ Asset Manager / Processor / Supervisor

**Title / Role**

Phase III
Structuring→ Asset Manager / Special Assets / Workout Officer / Etc.

→ Asset Manager / Special Assets / Workout Officer / Etc.

**Method**

→ Phone / Email / Portal Message / In Person

**Summary of Discussion**

→ Objective summary only

**Commitments Made**

→ What lender agreed to (if anything)

**Follow-Up Required**

→ What operator must provide

**Next Action Date**

→ Deadline for next touchpoint

**ESCALATION NOTE SECTION**

Escalation Trigger Identified:

___

___

___

___

Supervisor Contact Initiated?

□ Yes

□ No

Date of Escalation:

___

**COMMUNICATION PATTERN REVIEW**

Response Time Trend:

□ Prompt

□ Moderate Delay

□ Slow / Non-Responsive

Communication Tone Observed:

□ Cooperative

□ Neutral

□ Defensive

□ Adversarial

Is Relationship Improving?

□ Yes

□ No

□ Stalled

**CONTROL CONFIRMATION**

Last Confirmed File Status:

___

Next Required Submission Date:

___

Operator Initials:

___

Date:

# Lender Communication Log

Document all material communication with lender representatives.

Record factual content only. Avoid interpretation or opinion.

---

## COMMUNICATION LOG TABLE

| Date | Contact Name | Title / Role | Method | Summary of Discussion | Commitments Made | Follow-Up Required | Next Action Date |
|---|---|---|---|---|---|---|---|
| | | | | | | | |
| | | | | | | | |
| | | | | | | | |
| | | | | | | | |
| | | | | | | | |
| | | | | | | | |
| | | | | | | | |
| | | | | | | | |
| | | | | | | | |
| | | | | | | | |
| | | | | | | | |
| | | | | | | | |

**Column Definitions**

**Date**

→ Calendar date

**Contact Name**

→ Asset Manager / Processor / Supervisor

**Title / Role**

→ Asset Manager / Special Assets / Workout Officer / Etc.

**Method**

→ Phone / Email / Portal Message / In Person

**Summary of Discussion**

→ Objective summary only

**Commitments Made**

→ What lender agreed to (if anything)

**Follow-Up Required**

→ What operator must provide

**Next Action Date**

→ Deadline for next touchpoint

## ESCALATION NOTE SECTION

Escalation Trigger Identified:

______________________________________________

______________________________________________

______________________________________________

______________________________________________

Supervisor Contact Initiated?

□ Yes
□ No

Date of Escalation:

______________________________________________

## COMMUNICATION PATTERN REVIEW

Response Time Trend:

□ Prompt
□ Moderate Delay
□ Slow / Non-Responsive

Communication Tone Observed:

□ Cooperative
□ Neutral
□ Defensive
□ Adversarial

Is Relationship Improving?

□ Yes
□ No
□ Stalled

## CONTROL CONFIRMATION

Last Confirmed File Status:

______________________________________________

Next Required Submission Date:

______________________________________________

Operator Initials:

______________________________________________

Phase III
StructuringDate:

Date:

---

# Escalation & Supervisor Tracking Log

Document all supervisory escalation efforts and related responses.
Escalate based on documented delay, inconsistency, or procedural breakdown.

## ESCALATION TRIGGER IDENTIFICATION

Reason for Escalation:

- □ No Response > 10 Business Days
- □ Conflicting Information
- □ Repeated Document Loss
- □ Procedural Non-Compliance
- □ Unreasonable Condition Imposed
- □ Foreclosure Timeline Conflict
- □ Other

Date Trigger Identified:

---

Supporting Evidence Logged?

- □ Yes
- □ No

Reference to Communication Log Entry:

---

## SUPERVISOR CONTACT TABLE

| Date | Supervisor Name | Title / Authority Level | Method | Issue Presented | Response Given | Commitment Made | Follow-Up Date |
|---|---|---|---|---|---|---|---|
| | | | | | | | |
| | | | | | | | |
| | | | | | | | |
| | | | | | | | |
| | | | | | | | |
| | | | | | | | |
| | | | | | | | |
| | | | | | | | |

Phase III
Structuring

| Date | Supervisor Name | Title / Authority Level | Method | Issue Presented | Response Given | Commitment Made | Follow-Up Date |
|---|---|---|---|---|---|---|---|
| | | | | | | | |
| | | | | | | | |
| | | | | | | | |
| | | | | | | | |

**ESCALATION OUTCOME TRACKING**

Did Escalation Resolve Issue?

- □ Yes
- □ Partially
- □ No

Was File Reassigned?

- □ Yes
- □ No

Was Credit Committee Review Accelerated?

- □ Yes
- □ No

Were New Conditions Imposed?

- □ Yes
- □ No

Details:

______________________________________________________________________

______________________________________________________________________

**MULTI-LEVEL ESCALATION TRACKING**

Second-Level Escalation Initiated?

- □ Yes
- □ No

Regional / Executive Contact Engaged?

- □ Yes
- □ No

Outside Counsel Involved?

- □ Yes
- □ No

Regulatory Complaint Considered?

- □ Yes
- □ No

Date of Highest-Level Contact:

______________________________________________________________________

## ESCALATION STRATEGY REVIEW

Was Escalation Premature?

- □ Yes
- □ No

Did Escalation Damage Relationship?

- □ Yes
- □ No
- □ Unclear

Was Leverage Increased?

- □ Yes
- □ No

Operator Notes:

______________________________________________

______________________________________________

## CONTROL CONFIRMATION

Current File Status After Escalation:

______________________________________________

Next Required Action:

______________________________________________

Reviewed By:

______________________________________________

Date:

______________________________________________

# Escalation & Supervisor Tracking Log

Document all supervisory escalation efforts and related responses.
Escalate based on documented delay, inconsistency, or procedural breakdown.

## ESCALATION TRIGGER IDENTIFICATION

Reason for Escalation:

- □ No Response > 10 Business Days
- □ Conflicting Information
- □ Repeated Document Loss
- □ Procedural Non-Compliance
- □ Unreasonable Condition Imposed
- □ Foreclosure Timeline Conflict
- □ Other

Date Trigger Identified:

___

Supporting Evidence Logged?

- □ Yes
- □ No

Reference to Communication Log Entry:

___

## SUPERVISOR CONTACT TABLE

| Date | Supervisor Name | Title / Authority Level | Method | Issue Presented | Response Given | Commitment Made | Follow-Up Date |
|---|---|---|---|---|---|---|---|
| | | | | | | | |
| | | | | | | | |
| | | | | | | | |
| | | | | | | | |
| | | | | | | | |
| | | | | | | | |
| | | | | | | | |
| | | | | | | | |

| Date | Supervisor Name | Title / Authority Level | Method | Issue Presented | Response Given | Commitment Made | Follow-Up Date |
|---|---|---|---|---|---|---|---|
| | | | | | | | |
| | | | | | | | |
| | | | | | | | |
| | | | | | | | |

## ESCALATION OUTCOME TRACKING

Did Escalation Resolve Issue?

□ Yes

□ Partially

□ No

Was File Reassigned?

□ Yes

□ No

Was Credit Committee Review Accelerated?

□ Yes

□ No

Were New Conditions Imposed?

□ Yes

□ No

Details:

______________________________________________

______________________________________________

## MULTI-LEVEL ESCALATION TRACKING

Second-Level Escalation Initiated?

□ Yes

□ No

Regional / Executive Contact Engaged?

□ Yes

□ No

Outside Counsel Involved?

□ Yes

□ No

Regulatory Complaint Considered?

□ Yes

□ No

Date of Highest-Level Contact:

______________________________________________

## ESCALATION STRATEGY REVIEW

Was Escalation Premature?

- □ Yes
- □ No

Did Escalation Damage Relationship?

- □ Yes
- □ No
- □ Unclear

Was Leverage Increased?

- □ Yes
- □ No

Operator Notes:

____________________________________________________________

____________________________________________________________

## CONTROL CONFIRMATION

Current File Status After Escalation:

____________________________________________________________

Next Required Action:

____________________________________________________________

Reviewed By:

____________________________________________________________

Date:

____________________________________________________________

# Escalation & Supervisor Tracking Log

Document all supervisory escalation efforts and related responses.
Escalate based on documented delay, inconsistency, or procedural breakdown.

**ESCALATION TRIGGER IDENTIFICATION**

Reason for Escalation:

- ☐ No Response > 10 Business Days
- ☐ Conflicting Information
- ☐ Repeated Document Loss
- ☐ Procedural Non-Compliance
- ☐ Unreasonable Condition Imposed
- ☐ Foreclosure Timeline Conflict
- ☐ Other

Date Trigger Identified:

---

Supporting Evidence Logged?

- ☐ Yes
- ☐ No

Reference to Communication Log Entry:

---

**SUPERVISOR CONTACT TABLE**

| Date | Supervisor Name | Title / Authority Level | Method | Issue Presented | Response Given | Commitment Made | Follow-Up Date |
|---|---|---|---|---|---|---|---|
| | | | | | | | |
| | | | | | | | |
| | | | | | | | |
| | | | | | | | |
| | | | | | | | |
| | | | | | | | |
| | | | | | | | |
| | | | | | | | |

Phase III
Structuring

| Date | Supervisor Name | Title / Authority Level | Method | Issue Presented | Response Given | Commitment Made | Follow-Up Date |
|---|---|---|---|---|---|---|---|
| | | | | | | | |
| | | | | | | | |
| | | | | | | | |
| | | | | | | | |

**ESCALATION OUTCOME TRACKING**

Did Escalation Resolve Issue?
- □ Yes
- □ Partially
- □ No

Was File Reassigned?
- □ Yes
- □ No

Was Credit Committee Review Accelerated?
- □ Yes
- □ No

Were New Conditions Imposed?
- □ Yes
- □ No

Details:

---

---

**MULTI-LEVEL ESCALATION TRACKING**

Second-Level Escalation Initiated?
- □ Yes
- □ No

Regional / Executive Contact Engaged?
- □ Yes
- □ No

Outside Counsel Involved?
- □ Yes
- □ No

Regulatory Complaint Considered?
- □ Yes
- □ No

Date of Highest-Level Contact:

---

## ESCALATION STRATEGY REVIEW

Was Escalation Premature?

- □ Yes
- □ No

Did Escalation Damage Relationship?

- □ Yes
- □ No
- □ Unclear

Was Leverage Increased?

- □ Yes
- □ No

Operator Notes:

____________________________________________________________

____________________________________________________________

## CONTROL CONFIRMATION

Current File Status After Escalation:

____________________________________________________________

Next Required Action:

____________________________________________________________

Reviewed By:

____________________________________________________________

Date:

____________________________________________________________

## Escalation & Supervisor Tracking Log

Document all supervisory escalation efforts and related responses.
Escalate based on documented delay, inconsistency, or procedural breakdown.

### ESCALATION TRIGGER IDENTIFICATION

Reason for Escalation:

- □ No Response > 10 Business Days
- □ Conflicting Information
- □ Repeated Document Loss
- □ Procedural Non-Compliance
- □ Unreasonable Condition Imposed
- □ Foreclosure Timeline Conflict
- □ Other

Date Trigger Identified:

___

Supporting Evidence Logged?

- □ Yes
- □ No

Reference to Communication Log Entry:

___

### SUPERVISOR CONTACT TABLE

| Date | Supervisor Name | Title / Authority Level | Method | Issue Presented | Response Given | Commitment Made | Follow-Up Date |
|---|---|---|---|---|---|---|---|
| | | | | | | | |
| | | | | | | | |
| | | | | | | | |
| | | | | | | | |
| | | | | | | | |
| | | | | | | | |
| | | | | | | | |
| | | | | | | | |

| Date | Supervisor Name | Title / Authority Level | Method | Issue Presented | Response Given | Commitment Made | Follow-Up Date |
|---|---|---|---|---|---|---|---|
| | | | | | | | |
| | | | | | | | |
| | | | | | | | |
| | | | | | | | |

## ESCALATION OUTCOME TRACKING

Did Escalation Resolve Issue?

- □ Yes
- □ Partially
- □ No

Was File Reassigned?

- □ Yes
- □ No

Was Credit Committee Review Accelerated?

- □ Yes
- □ No

Were New Conditions Imposed?

- □ Yes
- □ No

Details:

______________________________________________

______________________________________________

## MULTI-LEVEL ESCALATION TRACKING

Second-Level Escalation Initiated?

- □ Yes
- □ No

Regional / Executive Contact Engaged?

- □ Yes
- □ No

Outside Counsel Involved?

- □ Yes
- □ No

Regulatory Complaint Considered?

- □ Yes
- □ No

Date of Highest-Level Contact:

______________________________________________

## ESCALATION STRATEGY REVIEW

Was Escalation Premature?

- □ Yes
- □ No

Did Escalation Damage Relationship?

- □ Yes
- □ No
- □ Unclear

Was Leverage Increased?

- □ Yes
- □ No

Operator Notes:

______________________________________________________________________

______________________________________________________________________

## CONTROL CONFIRMATION

Current File Status After Escalation:

______________________________________________________________________

Next Required Action:

______________________________________________________________________

Reviewed By:

______________________________________________________________________

Date:

______________________________________________________________________

# Escalation & Supervisor Tracking Log

Document all supervisory escalation efforts and related responses.
Escalate based on documented delay, inconsistency, or procedural breakdown.

## ESCALATION TRIGGER IDENTIFICATION

Reason for Escalation:

- □ No Response > 10 Business Days
- □ Conflicting Information
- □ Repeated Document Loss
- □ Procedural Non-Compliance
- □ Unreasonable Condition Imposed
- □ Foreclosure Timeline Conflict
- □ Other

Date Trigger Identified:

______________________________

Supporting Evidence Logged?

- □ Yes
- □ No

Reference to Communication Log Entry:

______________________________

## SUPERVISOR CONTACT TABLE

| Date | Supervisor Name | Title / Authority Level | Method | Issue Presented | Response Given | Commitment Made | Follow-Up Date |
|---|---|---|---|---|---|---|---|
| | | | | | | | |
| | | | | | | | |
| | | | | | | | |
| | | | | | | | |
| | | | | | | | |
| | | | | | | | |
| | | | | | | | |
| | | | | | | | |

Phase III
Structuring

| Date | Supervisor Name | Title / Authority Level | Method | Issue Presented | Response Given | Commitment Made | Follow-Up Date |
|---|---|---|---|---|---|---|---|
| | | | | | | | |
| | | | | | | | |
| | | | | | | | |
| | | | | | | | |

## ESCALATION OUTCOME TRACKING

Did Escalation Resolve Issue?

- □ Yes
- □ Partially
- □ No

Was File Reassigned?

- □ Yes
- □ No

Was Credit Committee Review Accelerated?

- □ Yes
- □ No

Were New Conditions Imposed?

- □ Yes
- □ No

Details:

________________________________________________

________________________________________________

## MULTI-LEVEL ESCALATION TRACKING

Second-Level Escalation Initiated?

- □ Yes
- □ No

Regional / Executive Contact Engaged?

- □ Yes
- □ No

Outside Counsel Involved?

- □ Yes
- □ No

Regulatory Complaint Considered?

- □ Yes
- □ No

Date of Highest-Level Contact:

________________________________________________

## ESCALATION STRATEGY REVIEW

Was Escalation Premature?

- □ Yes
- □ No

Did Escalation Damage Relationship?

- □ Yes
- □ No
- □ Unclear

Was Leverage Increased?

- □ Yes
- □ No

Operator Notes:

______________________________________________________________________

______________________________________________________________________

## CONTROL CONFIRMATION

Current File Status After Escalation:

______________________________________________________________________

Next Required Action:

______________________________________________________________________

Reviewed By:

______________________________________________________________________

Date:

______________________________________________________________________

# BPO Challenge Worksheet

Document discrepancies between lender-ordered BPO and supported market data.
Support all challenges with objective evidence and comparable sales documentation.

**BPO SUMMARY**

BPO Value Indicated:

______________________________________________

Date of BPO:

______________________________________________

BPO Agent / Broker:

______________________________________________

Property Inspection Conducted?

- □ Yes
- □ No
- □ Unknown

BPO Type:

- □ Exterior Only
- □ Interior
- □ Hybrid

**VALUE VARIANCE ANALYSIS**

Selected Working Value (Internal):

______________________________________________

Difference Between BPO and Internal Value:

______________________________________________

Variance %:

______________________________________________

Is Variance Material?

- □ Yes
- □ No

**COMPARABLE SALE DISCREPANCIES**

Did BPO Use Comparable Sales Outside Submarket?

- □ Yes
- □ No

Did BPO Use Sales Outside 6–12 Months?

- □ Yes
- □ No

Did BPO Ignore Recent Lower Sales?

- □ Yes
- □ No

Are Size Adjustments Unrealistic?

- □ Yes
- □ No

Are Condition Adjustments Inadequate?

□ Yes
□ No

Details:

---

---

**CONDITION MISREPRESENTATION**

Did BPO Overlook Deferred Maintenance?

□ Yes
□ No

Were Repairs Underestimated?

□ Yes
□ No

Is Inspection Report Attached to Challenge?

□ Yes
□ No

Repair Cost Documentation Included?

□ Yes
□ No

**MARKET CONDITION ERRORS**

Is Cap Rate Assumption Unrealistic?

□ Yes
□ No

Does BPO Reflect Current Market Softness?

□ Yes
□ No

Are Active Listings Being Used Instead of Closed Sales?

□ Yes
□ No

Is Time Adjustment Missing?

□ Yes
□ No

Details:

---

---

**FORMAL CHALLENGE COMPONENTS**

Comparable Sales Package Prepared?

□ Yes
□ No

Repair Estimates Attached?

□ Yes
□ No

Market Narrative Prepared?

□ Yes
□ No

Phase III
StructuringRevised Net-to-Lender Analysis Updated?

Revised Net-to-Lender Analysis Updated?

- □ Yes
- □ No

Date Challenge Submitted:

___

**LENDER RESPONSE TRACKING**

Date Response Received:

___

BPO Revised?

- □ Yes
- □ No

New Value Indicated:

___

Was Credit Committee Notified?

- □ Yes
- □ No

**CHALLENGE OUTCOME**

Was Value Adjustment Granted?

- □ Yes
- □ No

Impact on Short Sale Feasibility:

___

Next Strategic Step:

___

Operator Notes:

___

___

# Valuation Dispute Documentation Log

Document all valuation discrepancies, challenges, revisions, and lender responses.
Maintain objective record of data submitted and outcomes received.

**VALUATION EVENT LOG TABLE**

| Date | Valuation Source | Value Indicated | Basis of Valuation | Dispute Reason | Evidence Submitted | Lender Response | Revised Value | Satatus |
|---|---|---|---|---|---|---|---|---|
| | | | | | | | | |
| | | | | | | | | |
| | | | | | | | | |
| | | | | | | | | |
| | | | | | | | | |
| | | | | | | | | |
| | | | | | | | | |
| | | | | | | | | |
| | | | | | | | | |
| | | | | | | | | |
| | | | | | | | | |
| | | | | | | | | |
| | | | | | | | | |
| | | | | | | | | |
| | | | | | | | | |

**Date**

→ Date dispute initiated or new valuation received

Valuation Source

→ BPO / Appraisal / Internal Review / Credit Committee / REO Dept.

**Value Indicated**

→ Dollar amount

**Basis of Valuation**

→ Sales Comp / Income Approach / Hybrid

**Dispute Reason**

→ Overstated comps / Condition ignored / Cap rate error / Etc.

**Evidence Submitted**

→ Comps / Repair Estimates / Market Report / Photos

**Lender Response**

→ Accepted / Rejected / Partial / No Response

**Revised Value**

→ If adjusted

**Status**

→ Open / Closed / Escalated / Pending

**SUPPORTING DOCUMENTATION TRACKING**

Comparable Package Submitted?

□ Yes

□ No

Repair Estimates Submitted?

□ Yes

□ No

Updated Net-to-Lender Model Submitted?

□ Yes

□ No

Market Condition Narrative Submitted?

□ Yes

□ No

Date of Most Recent Valuation Submission:

---

**ESCALATION LINKAGE**

Was Escalation Triggered by Valuation Dispute?

□ Yes

□ No

Supervisor Notified?

□ Yes

□ No

Credit Committee Review Requested?

□ Yes

□ No

**TREND ANALYSIS**

Is Lender Moving Toward Market Reality?

- □ Yes
- □ No
- □ Uncertain

Has Value Drifted Over Time?

- □ Upward
- □ Downward
- □ Stable

Is Dispute Economically Material?

- □ Yes
- □ No

Operator Notes:

___

___

# Valuation Dispute Documentation Log

Document all valuation discrepancies, challenges, revisions, and lender responses.
Maintain objective record of data submitted and outcomes received.

**VALUATION EVENT LOG TABLE**

| Date | Valuation Source | Value Indicated | Basis of Valuation | Dispute Reason | Evidence Submitted | Lender Response | Revised Value | Satatus |
|---|---|---|---|---|---|---|---|---|
| | | | | | | | | |
| | | | | | | | | |
| | | | | | | | | |
| | | | | | | | | |
| | | | | | | | | |
| | | | | | | | | |
| | | | | | | | | |
| | | | | | | | | |
| | | | | | | | | |
| | | | | | | | | |
| | | | | | | | | |
| | | | | | | | | |
| | | | | | | | | |
| | | | | | | | | |
| | | | | | | | | |

**Date**

→ Date dispute initiated or new valuation received

Valuation Source

→ BPO / Appraisal / Internal Review / Credit Committee / REO Dept.

**Value Indicated**

→ Dollar amount

**Basis of Valuation**

→ Sales Comp / Income Approach / Hybrid

**Dispute Reason**

→ Overstated comps / Condition ignored / Cap rate error / Etc.

**Evidence Submitted**

→ Comps / Repair Estimates / Market Report / Photos

**Lender Response**

→ Accepted / Rejected / Partial / No Response

**Revised Value**

→ If adjusted

**Status**

→ Open / Closed / Escalated / Pending

**SUPPORTING DOCUMENTATION TRACKING**

Comparable Package Submitted?

□ Yes

□ No

Repair Estimates Submitted?

□ Yes

□ No

Updated Net-to-Lender Model Submitted?

□ Yes

□ No

Market Condition Narrative Submitted?

□ Yes

□ No

Date of Most Recent Valuation Submission:

---

**ESCALATION LINKAGE**

Was Escalation Triggered by Valuation Dispute?

□ Yes

□ No

Supervisor Notified?

□ Yes

□ No

Credit Committee Review Requested?

□ Yes

□ No

**TREND ANALYSIS**

Is Lender Moving Toward Market Reality?

- □ Yes
- □ No
- □ Uncertain

Has Value Drifted Over Time?

- □ Upward
- □ Downward
- □ Stable

Is Dispute Economically Material?

- □ Yes
- □ No

Operator Notes:

# Valuation Dispute Documentation Log

Document all valuation discrepancies, challenges, revisions, and lender responses.
Maintain objective record of data submitted and outcomes received.

**VALUATION EVENT LOG TABLE**

| Date | Valuation Source | Value Indicated | Basis of Valuation | Dispute Reason | Evidence Submitted | Lender Response | Revised Value | Satatus |
|---|---|---|---|---|---|---|---|---|
| | | | | | | | | |
| | | | | | | | | |
| | | | | | | | | |
| | | | | | | | | |
| | | | | | | | | |
| | | | | | | | | |
| | | | | | | | | |
| | | | | | | | | |
| | | | | | | | | |
| | | | | | | | | |
| | | | | | | | | |
| | | | | | | | | |
| | | | | | | | | |
| | | | | | | | | |
| | | | | | | | | |

Phase III
StructuringDate

**Date**

→ Date dispute initiated or new valuation received

Valuation Source

→ BPO / Appraisal / Internal Review / Credit Committee / REO Dept.

**Value Indicated**

→ Dollar amount

**Basis of Valuation**

→ Sales Comp / Income Approach / Hybrid

**Dispute Reason**

→ Overstated comps / Condition ignored / Cap rate error / Etc.

**Evidence Submitted**

→ Comps / Repair Estimates / Market Report / Photos

**Lender Response**

→ Accepted / Rejected / Partial / No Response

**Revised Value**

→ If adjusted

**Status**

→ Open / Closed / Escalated / Pending

**SUPPORTING DOCUMENTATION TRACKING**

Comparable Package Submitted?

□ Yes
□ No

Repair Estimates Submitted?

□ Yes
□ No

Updated Net-to-Lender Model Submitted?

□ Yes
□ No

Market Condition Narrative Submitted?

□ Yes
□ No

Date of Most Recent Valuation Submission:

---

**ESCALATION LINKAGE**

Was Escalation Triggered by Valuation Dispute?

□ Yes
□ No

Supervisor Notified?

□ Yes
□ No

Credit Committee Review Requested?

□ Yes
□ No

**TREND ANALYSIS**

Is Lender Moving Toward Market Reality?

- □ Yes
- □ No
- □ Uncertain

Has Value Drifted Over Time?

- □ Upward
- □ Downward
- □ Stable

Is Dispute Economically Material?

- □ Yes
- □ No

Operator Notes:

______________________________________________________________________

______________________________________________________________________

# Valuation Dispute Documentation Log

Document all valuation discrepancies, challenges, revisions, and lender responses.
Maintain objective record of data submitted and outcomes received.

**VALUATION EVENT LOG TABLE**

| Date | Valuation Source | Value Indicated | Basis of Valuation | Dispute Reason | Evidence Submitted | Lender Response | Revised Value | Satatus |
|---|---|---|---|---|---|---|---|---|
| | | | | | | | | |
| | | | | | | | | |
| | | | | | | | | |
| | | | | | | | | |
| | | | | | | | | |
| | | | | | | | | |
| | | | | | | | | |
| | | | | | | | | |
| | | | | | | | | |
| | | | | | | | | |
| | | | | | | | | |
| | | | | | | | | |
| | | | | | | | | |
| | | | | | | | | |
| | | | | | | | | |

**Date**

→ Date dispute initiated or new valuation received

Valuation Source

→ BPO / Appraisal / Internal Review / Credit Committee / REO Dept.

**Value Indicated**

→ Dollar amount

**Basis of Valuation**

→ Sales Comp / Income Approach / Hybrid

**Dispute Reason**

→ Overstated comps / Condition ignored / Cap rate error / Etc.

**Evidence Submitted**

→ Comps / Repair Estimates / Market Report / Photos

**Lender Response**

→ Accepted / Rejected / Partial / No Response

**Revised Value**

→ If adjusted

**Status**

→ Open / Closed / Escalated / Pending

**SUPPORTING DOCUMENTATION TRACKING**

Comparable Package Submitted?

□ Yes

□ No

Repair Estimates Submitted?

□ Yes

□ No

Updated Net-to-Lender Model Submitted?

□ Yes

□ No

Market Condition Narrative Submitted?

□ Yes

□ No

Date of Most Recent Valuation Submission:

---

**ESCALATION LINKAGE**

Was Escalation Triggered by Valuation Dispute?

□ Yes

□ No

Supervisor Notified?

□ Yes

□ No

Credit Committee Review Requested?

□ Yes

□ No

**TREND ANALYSIS**

Is Lender Moving Toward Market Reality?

- □ Yes
- □ No
- □ Uncertain

Has Value Drifted Over Time?

- □ Upward
- □ Downward
- □ Stable

Is Dispute Economically Material?

- □ Yes
- □ No

Operator Notes:

___

___

# Valuation Dispute Documentation Log

Document all valuation discrepancies, challenges, revisions, and lender responses.
Maintain objective record of data submitted and outcomes received.

**VALUATION EVENT LOG TABLE**

| Date | Valuation Source | Value Indicated | Basis of Valuation | Dispute Reason | Evidence Submitted | Lender Response | Revised Value | Satatus |
|---|---|---|---|---|---|---|---|---|
| | | | | | | | | |
| | | | | | | | | |
| | | | | | | | | |
| | | | | | | | | |
| | | | | | | | | |
| | | | | | | | | |
| | | | | | | | | |
| | | | | | | | | |
| | | | | | | | | |
| | | | | | | | | |
| | | | | | | | | |
| | | | | | | | | |
| | | | | | | | | |
| | | | | | | | | |
| | | | | | | | | |

Phase III
StructuringDate

**Date**

→ Date dispute initiated or new valuation received

Valuation Source

→ BPO / Appraisal / Internal Review / Credit Committee / REO Dept.

**Value Indicated**

→ Dollar amount

**Basis of Valuation**

→ Sales Comp / Income Approach / Hybrid

**Dispute Reason**

→ Overstated comps / Condition ignored / Cap rate error / Etc.

**Evidence Submitted**

→ Comps / Repair Estimates / Market Report / Photos

**Lender Response**

→ Accepted / Rejected / Partial / No Response

**Revised Value**

→ If adjusted

**Status**

→ Open / Closed / Escalated / Pending

**SUPPORTING DOCUMENTATION TRACKING**

Comparable Package Submitted?

□ Yes
□ No

Repair Estimates Submitted?

□ Yes
□ No

Updated Net-to-Lender Model Submitted?

□ Yes
□ No

Market Condition Narrative Submitted?

□ Yes
□ No

Date of Most Recent Valuation Submission:

---

**ESCALATION LINKAGE**

Was Escalation Triggered by Valuation Dispute?

□ Yes
□ No

Supervisor Notified?

□ Yes
□ No

Credit Committee Review Requested?

□ Yes
□ No

**TREND ANALYSIS**

Is Lender Moving Toward Market Reality?

□ Yes

□ No

□ Uncertain

Has Value Drifted Over Time?

□ Upward

□ Downward

□ Stable

Is Dispute Economically Material?

□ Yes

□ No

Operator Notes:

______________________________________________________________________

______________________________________________________________________

# Valuation Dispute Documentation Log

Document all valuation discrepancies, challenges, revisions, and lender responses.
Maintain objective record of data submitted and outcomes received.

**VALUATION EVENT LOG TABLE**

| Date | Valuation Source | Value Indicated | Basis of Valuation | Dispute Reason | Evidence Submitted | Lender Response | Revised Value | Satatus |
|---|---|---|---|---|---|---|---|---|
| | | | | | | | | |
| | | | | | | | | |
| | | | | | | | | |
| | | | | | | | | |
| | | | | | | | | |
| | | | | | | | | |
| | | | | | | | | |
| | | | | | | | | |
| | | | | | | | | |
| | | | | | | | | |
| | | | | | | | | |
| | | | | | | | | |
| | | | | | | | | |
| | | | | | | | | |
| | | | | | | | | |

**Date**

→ Date dispute initiated or new valuation received

Valuation Source

→ BPO / Appraisal / Internal Review / Credit Committee / REO Dept.

**Value Indicated**

→ Dollar amount

**Basis of Valuation**

→ Sales Comp / Income Approach / Hybrid

**Dispute Reason**

→ Overstated comps / Condition ignored / Cap rate error / Etc.

**Evidence Submitted**

→ Comps / Repair Estimates / Market Report / Photos

**Lender Response**

→ Accepted / Rejected / Partial / No Response

**Revised Value**

→ If adjusted

**Status**

→ Open / Closed / Escalated / Pending

**SUPPORTING DOCUMENTATION TRACKING**

Comparable Package Submitted?

□ Yes

□ No

Repair Estimates Submitted?

□ Yes

□ No

Updated Net-to-Lender Model Submitted?

□ Yes

□ No

Market Condition Narrative Submitted?

□ Yes

□ No

Date of Most Recent Valuation Submission:

---

**ESCALATION LINKAGE**

Was Escalation Triggered by Valuation Dispute?

□ Yes

□ No

Supervisor Notified?

□ Yes

□ No

Credit Committee Review Requested?

□ Yes

□ No

**TREND ANALYSIS**

Is Lender Moving Toward Market Reality?

- □ Yes
- □ No
- □ Uncertain

Has Value Drifted Over Time?

- □ Upward
- □ Downward
- □ Stable

Is Dispute Economically Material?

- □ Yes
- □ No

Operator Notes:

______________________________________________________________________

______________________________________________________________________

# Junior Lien Negotiation Tracker

Track negotiation activity and settlement positioning with subordinate lienholders.
Document economic leverage and settlement progression objectively.

## JUNIOR LIEN PROFILE

Junior Lienholder Name:

---

Position (2nd / 3rd / Mezz / HOA / Other):

---

Original Loan Amount:

---

Current Claimed Balance:

---

Estimated Collateral Value Coverage:

---

Is Junior In-the-Money?

- □ Yes
- □ No
- □ Marginal

Recourse Exposure:

- □ Yes
- □ No
- □ Unknown

## INTERCREDITOR POSITION

Intercreditor Agreement Identified?

- □ Yes
- □ No

Standstill Provisions Known?

- □ Yes
- □ No

Blockage Rights?

- □ Yes
- □ No

Consent Required for Short Sale?

- □ Yes
- □ No

Is Junior Economically Impaired?

- □ Yes
- □ No

## NEGOTIATION LOG TABLE

| Date | Contact Name | Offer Made | Counter Demand | Settlement Rate | Leverage Position | Status | Next Action |
|---|---|---|---|---|---|---|---|
| | | | | | | | |
| | | | | | | | |
| | | | | | | | |
| | | | | | | | |
| | | | | | | | |
| | | | | | | | |
| | | | | | | | |
| | | | | | | | |
| | | | | | | | |
| | | | | | | | |
| | | | | | | | |
| | | | | | | | |
| | | | | | | | |

## SETTLEMENT STRUCTURE ANALYSIS

Initial Settlement Offer:

___

Highest Junior Demand:

___

Current Negotiation Range:

___

Cash Contribution Proposed by Buyer:

Contribution Requested from Borrower:

___

Is Release of Lien Confirmed?

□ Yes

□ No

Is Deficiency Waiver Requested?

□ Yes

□ No

## LEVERAGE ASSESSMENT

Junior Leverage Source:

□ Legal Priority

□ Consent Requirement

□ Emotional / Nuisance

□ Recourse Threat

□ Litigation Threat

□ Other

Is Junior Willing to Litigate?

□ Yes

□ No

□ Bluff Suspected

Is Time Working Against Junior?

□ Yes

□ No

## ESCALATION & STRATEGY

Escalation to Supervisor Required?

□ Yes

□ No

Is Senior Lender Supporting Settlement Pressure?

□ Yes

□ No

Is File at Risk Due to Junior Holdout?

□ Yes

□ No

Next Strategic Move:

______________________________________________________________

______________________________________________________________

**OUTCOME SUMMARY**

Final Settlement Amount:

______________________________________________

Date Settlement Reached:

______________________________________________

Lien Release Confirmed?

- □ Yes
- □ No

Deficiency Released?

- □ Yes
- □ No

Operator Notes:

______________________________________________

______________________________________________

# Counteroffer & Concession Log

Document all counteroffers, concessions, and structural adjustments during negotiation. Track economic movement and cumulative impact on net recovery.

## COUNTEROFFER TRACKING TABLE

| Date | Party Initiating | Offer Price | Cash Contribution | Repair Credit | Timeline Change | Dificiency Treatment | Net to Lender Impact | Status | Notes |
|---|---|---|---|---|---|---|---|---|---|
| | | | | | | | | | |
| | | | | | | | | | |
| | | | | | | | | | |
| | | | | | | | | | |
| | | | | | | | | | |
| | | | | | | | | | |
| | | | | | | | | | |
| | | | | | | | | | |
| | | | | | | | | | |
| | | | | | | | | | |
| | | | | | | | | | |
| | | | | | | | | | |
| | | | | | | | | | |

**Column Definitions**

**Date**

→ Calendar date

**Party Initiating**

→ Senior Lender / Junior Lender / Buyer / Borrower

**Offer Price**
→ Dollar amount
**Cash Contribution**
→ Additional cash required from buyer or borrower
**Repair Credit**
→ Adjustment amount
**Timeline Change**
→ Revised closing date or deadline
**Deficiency Treatment**
→ Full release / Partial release / Contribution required
**Net-to-Lender Impact**
→ Increase / Decrease / Neutral (brief note)
**Status**
→ Pending / Accepted / Rejected / Superseded
**Notes**
→ Brief factual summary

**CUMULATIVE CONCESSION SUMMARY**

Original Offer Price:

___

Current Working Price:

___

Total Buyer Concessions to Date:

___

Total Lender Concessions to Date:

___

Net Change from Initial Position:

___

Is Concession Drift Material?
□ Yes
□ No

**NEGOTIATION LEVERAGE REVIEW**

Is Leverage Increasing or Decreasing?
□ Increasing
□ Decreasing
□ Stable
Primary Pressure Driver:
□ Foreclosure Timeline
□ Accrual Growth
□ Credit Committee Review
□ Junior Holdout
□ Liquidity Pressure
□ Other
Are We Approaching Economic Limit?
□ Yes

□ No

**STRATEGIC CONTROL CHECK**

Has Original Strategy Shifted?

□ Yes

□ No

If Yes, Why:

---

Is File Still Within Kill Criteria?

□ Yes

□ No

Next Tactical Adjustment:

---

# Counteroffer & Concession Log

Document all counteroffers, concessions, and structural adjustments during negotiation. Track economic movement and cumulative impact on net recovery.

**COUNTEROFFER TRACKING TABLE**

| Date | Party Initiating | Offer Price | Cash Contribution | Repair Credit | Timeline Change | Dificiency Treatment | Net to Lender Impact | Status | Notes |
|---|---|---|---|---|---|---|---|---|---|
| | | | | | | | | | |
| | | | | | | | | | |
| | | | | | | | | | |
| | | | | | | | | | |
| | | | | | | | | | |
| | | | | | | | | | |
| | | | | | | | | | |
| | | | | | | | | | |
| | | | | | | | | | |
| | | | | | | | | | |
| | | | | | | | | | |
| | | | | | | | | | |
| | | | | | | | | | |

**Column Definitions**

**Date**

→ Calendar date

**Party Initiating**

→ Senior Lender / Junior Lender / Buyer / Borrower

**Offer Price**
→ Dollar amount
**Cash Contribution**
→ Additional cash required from buyer or borrower
**Repair Credit**
→ Adjustment amount
**Timeline Change**
→ Revised closing date or deadline
**Deficiency Treatment**
→ Full release / Partial release / Contribution required
**Net-to-Lender Impact**
→ Increase / Decrease / Neutral (brief note)
**Status**
→ Pending / Accepted / Rejected / Superseded
**Notes**
→ Brief factual summary

**CUMULATIVE CONCESSION SUMMARY**

Original Offer Price:

______________________________________________

Current Working Price:

______________________________________________

Total Buyer Concessions to Date:

______________________________________________

Total Lender Concessions to Date:

______________________________________________

Net Change from Initial Position:

______________________________________________

Is Concession Drift Material?
□ Yes
□ No

**NEGOTIATION LEVERAGE REVIEW**

Is Leverage Increasing or Decreasing?
□ Increasing
□ Decreasing
□ Stable
Primary Pressure Driver:
□ Foreclosure Timeline
□ Accrual Growth
□ Credit Committee Review
□ Junior Holdout
□ Liquidity Pressure
□ Other
Are We Approaching Economic Limit?
□ Yes

□ No

**STRATEGIC CONTROL CHECK**

Has Original Strategy Shifted?

□ Yes

□ No

If Yes, Why:

___

Is File Still Within Kill Criteria?

□ Yes

□ No

Next Tactical Adjustment:

___

# Counteroffer & Concession Log

Document all counteroffers, concessions, and structural adjustments during negotiation.
Track economic movement and cumulative impact on net recovery.

**COUNTEROFFER TRACKING TABLE**

| Date | Party Initiating | Offer Price | Cash Contribution | Repair Credit | Timeline Change | Dificiency Treatment | Net to Lender Impact | Status | Notes |
|---|---|---|---|---|---|---|---|---|---|
| | | | | | | | | | |
| | | | | | | | | | |
| | | | | | | | | | |
| | | | | | | | | | |
| | | | | | | | | | |
| | | | | | | | | | |
| | | | | | | | | | |
| | | | | | | | | | |
| | | | | | | | | | |
| | | | | | | | | | |
| | | | | | | | | | |
| | | | | | | | | | |
| | | | | | | | | | |

**Column Definitions**

**Date**

→ Calendar date

**Party Initiating**

→ Senior Lender / Junior Lender / Buyer / Borrower

**Offer Price**
→ Dollar amount
**Cash Contribution**
→ Additional cash required from buyer or borrower
**Repair Credit**
→ Adjustment amount
**Timeline Change**
→ Revised closing date or deadline
**Deficiency Treatment**
→ Full release / Partial release / Contribution required
**Net-to-Lender Impact**
→ Increase / Decrease / Neutral (brief note)
**Status**
→ Pending / Accepted / Rejected / Superseded
**Notes**
→ Brief factual summary

**CUMULATIVE CONCESSION SUMMARY**

Original Offer Price:

______________________________

Current Working Price:

______________________________

Total Buyer Concessions to Date:

______________________________

Total Lender Concessions to Date:

______________________________

Net Change from Initial Position:

______________________________

Is Concession Drift Material?
□ Yes
□ No

**NEGOTIATION LEVERAGE REVIEW**

Is Leverage Increasing or Decreasing?
□ Increasing
□ Decreasing
□ Stable

Primary Pressure Driver:
□ Foreclosure Timeline
□ Accrual Growth
□ Credit Committee Review
□ Junior Holdout
□ Liquidity Pressure
□ Other

Are We Approaching Economic Limit?
□ Yes

□ No

## STRATEGIC CONTROL CHECK

Has Original Strategy Shifted?

□ Yes

□ No

If Yes, Why:

______________________________________________________________________

Is File Still Within Kill Criteria?

□ Yes

□ No

Next Tactical Adjustment:

______________________________________________________________________

# Counteroffer & Concession Log

Document all counteroffers, concessions, and structural adjustments during negotiation.
Track economic movement and cumulative impact on net recovery.

**COUNTEROFFER TRACKING TABLE**

| Date | Party Initiating | Offer Price | Cash Contribution | Repair Credit | Timeline Change | Dificiency Treatment | Net to Lender Impact | Status | Notes |
|---|---|---|---|---|---|---|---|---|---|
| | | | | | | | | | |
| | | | | | | | | | |
| | | | | | | | | | |
| | | | | | | | | | |
| | | | | | | | | | |
| | | | | | | | | | |
| | | | | | | | | | |
| | | | | | | | | | |
| | | | | | | | | | |
| | | | | | | | | | |
| | | | | | | | | | |
| | | | | | | | | | |
| | | | | | | | | | |

**Column Definitions**

**Date**

→ Calendar date

**Party Initiating**

→ Senior Lender / Junior Lender / Buyer / Borrower

**Offer Price**
→ Dollar amount
**Cash Contribution**
→ Additional cash required from buyer or borrower
**Repair Credit**
→ Adjustment amount
**Timeline Change**
→ Revised closing date or deadline
**Deficiency Treatment**
→ Full release / Partial release / Contribution required
**Net-to-Lender Impact**
→ Increase / Decrease / Neutral (brief note)
**Status**
→ Pending / Accepted / Rejected / Superseded
**Notes**
→ Brief factual summary

**CUMULATIVE CONCESSION SUMMARY**

Original Offer Price:

___

Current Working Price:

___

Total Buyer Concessions to Date:

___

Total Lender Concessions to Date:

___

Net Change from Initial Position:

___

Is Concession Drift Material?
□ Yes
□ No

**NEGOTIATION LEVERAGE REVIEW**

Is Leverage Increasing or Decreasing?
□ Increasing
□ Decreasing
□ Stable

Primary Pressure Driver:
□ Foreclosure Timeline
□ Accrual Growth
□ Credit Committee Review
□ Junior Holdout
□ Liquidity Pressure
□ Other

Are We Approaching Economic Limit?
□ Yes

□ No

**STRATEGIC CONTROL CHECK**

Has Original Strategy Shifted?

□ Yes

□ No

If Yes, Why:

---

Is File Still Within Kill Criteria?

□ Yes

□ No

Next Tactical Adjustment:

---

# Counteroffer & Concession Log

Document all counteroffers, concessions, and structural adjustments during negotiation. Track economic movement and cumulative impact on net recovery.

## COUNTEROFFER TRACKING TABLE

| Date | Party Initiating | Offer Price | Cash Contribution | Repair Credit | Timeline Change | Dificiency Treatment | Net to Lender Impact | Status | Notes |
|---|---|---|---|---|---|---|---|---|---|
| | | | | | | | | | |
| | | | | | | | | | |
| | | | | | | | | | |
| | | | | | | | | | |
| | | | | | | | | | |
| | | | | | | | | | |
| | | | | | | | | | |
| | | | | | | | | | |
| | | | | | | | | | |
| | | | | | | | | | |
| | | | | | | | | | |
| | | | | | | | | | |
| | | | | | | | | | |

**Column Definitions**

**Date**

→ Calendar date

**Party Initiating**

→ Senior Lender / Junior Lender / Buyer / Borrower

**Offer Price**

→ Dollar amount

**Cash Contribution**

→ Additional cash required from buyer or borrower

**Repair Credit**

→ Adjustment amount

**Timeline Change**

→ Revised closing date or deadline

**Deficiency Treatment**

→ Full release / Partial release / Contribution required

**Net-to-Lender Impact**

→ Increase / Decrease / Neutral (brief note)

**Status**

→ Pending / Accepted / Rejected / Superseded

**Notes**

→ Brief factual summary

## CUMULATIVE CONCESSION SUMMARY

Original Offer Price:

______________________________________________

Current Working Price:

______________________________________________

Total Buyer Concessions to Date:

______________________________________________

Total Lender Concessions to Date:

______________________________________________

Net Change from Initial Position:

______________________________________________

Is Concession Drift Material?

□ Yes

□ No

## NEGOTIATION LEVERAGE REVIEW

Is Leverage Increasing or Decreasing?

□ Increasing

□ Decreasing

□ Stable

Primary Pressure Driver:

□ Foreclosure Timeline

□ Accrual Growth

□ Credit Committee Review

□ Junior Holdout

□ Liquidity Pressure

□ Other

Are We Approaching Economic Limit?

□ Yes

□ No

**STRATEGIC CONTROL CHECK**

Has Original Strategy Shifted?

□ Yes

□ No

If Yes, Why:

---

Is File Still Within Kill Criteria?

□ Yes

□ No

Next Tactical Adjustment:

---

## Counteroffer & Concession Log

Document all counteroffers, concessions, and structural adjustments during negotiation. Track economic movement and cumulative impact on net recovery.

**COUNTEROFFER TRACKING TABLE**

| Date | Party Initiating | Offer Price | Cash Contribution | Repair Credit | Timeline Change | Dificiency Treatment | Net to Lender Impact | Status | Notes |
|---|---|---|---|---|---|---|---|---|---|
| | | | | | | | | | |
| | | | | | | | | | |
| | | | | | | | | | |
| | | | | | | | | | |
| | | | | | | | | | |
| | | | | | | | | | |
| | | | | | | | | | |
| | | | | | | | | | |
| | | | | | | | | | |
| | | | | | | | | | |
| | | | | | | | | | |
| | | | | | | | | | |
| | | | | | | | | | |

**Column Definitions**

**Date**

→ Calendar date

**Party Initiating**

→ Senior Lender / Junior Lender / Buyer / Borrower

**Offer Price**
→ Dollar amount
**Cash Contribution**
→ Additional cash required from buyer or borrower
**Repair Credit**
→ Adjustment amount
**Timeline Change**
→ Revised closing date or deadline
**Deficiency Treatment**
→ Full release / Partial release / Contribution required
**Net-to-Lender Impact**
→ Increase / Decrease / Neutral (brief note)
**Status**
→ Pending / Accepted / Rejected / Superseded
**Notes**
→ Brief factual summary

**CUMULATIVE CONCESSION SUMMARY**

Original Offer Price:

_______________________________________________

Current Working Price:

_______________________________________________

Total Buyer Concessions to Date:

_______________________________________________

Total Lender Concessions to Date:

_______________________________________________

Net Change from Initial Position:

_______________________________________________

Is Concession Drift Material?
□ Yes
□ No

**NEGOTIATION LEVERAGE REVIEW**

Is Leverage Increasing or Decreasing?
□ Increasing
□ Decreasing
□ Stable
Primary Pressure Driver:
□ Foreclosure Timeline
□ Accrual Growth
□ Credit Committee Review
□ Junior Holdout
□ Liquidity Pressure
□ Other
Are We Approaching Economic Limit?
□ Yes

□ No

**STRATEGIC CONTROL CHECK**

Has Original Strategy Shifted?

□ Yes

□ No

If Yes, Why:

---

Is File Still Within Kill Criteria?

□ Yes

□ No

Next Tactical Adjustment:

---

# Timeline Compliance Tracker

Track all material deadlines, approval conditions, and foreclosure-related timelines.
Monitor compliance and identify time-sensitive risk exposure.

**MASTER DEADLINE TABLE**

| Deadline Type | Description | Responsible Party | Due Date | Days Remaining | Status | Risk Level | Extension Requested | Extension Granted | Notes |
|---|---|---|---|---|---|---|---|---|---|
| | | | | | | | | | |
| | | | | | | | | | |
| | | | | | | | | | |
| | | | | | | | | | |
| | | | | | | | | | |
| | | | | | | | | | |
| | | | | | | | | | |
| | | | | | | | | | |
| | | | | | | | | | |
| | | | | | | | | | |
| | | | | | | | | | |
| | | | | | | | | | |
| | | | | | | | | | |
| | | | | | | | | | |
| | | | | | | | | | |

Column Definitions

**Deadline Type**
→ Foreclosure Sale / Approval Expiration / Buyer Deposit / Lender Condition / Title Cure / Junior Consent / Other

**Description**
→ Specific requirement

**Responsible Party**
→ Buyer / Borrower / Senior Lender / Junior Lender / Title / Operator

**Due Date**
→ Calendar date

**Days Remaining**
→ Calculated manually or noted

**Status**
→ Pending / Complete / Overdue / Extended

**Risk Level**
→ Low / Moderate / High / Critical

**Extension Requested**
→ Yes / No

**Extension Granted**
→ Yes / No

**Notes**
→ Brief clarification

**FORECLOSURE TRACKING SECTION**

Current Foreclosure Sale Date:

_______________________________________________

Is Sale Date Confirmed?
- □ Yes
- □ No

Days Until Sale:

_______________________________________________

Has Sale Been Postponed?
- □ Yes
- □ No

Number of Postponements to Date:

_______________________________________________

Risk of Acceleration:
- □ Low
- □ Moderate
- □ High
- □ Immediate

## APPROVAL LETTER CONTROL

Short Sale Approval Date:

---

Approval Expiration Date:

---

Conditions Required Prior to Closing:

---

---

Are All Conditions Satisfied?

- □ Yes
- □ No

Remaining Conditions:

---

## BUYER PERFORMANCE MONITORING

Earnest Money Received?

- □ Yes
- □ No

Financing Approved?

- □ Yes
- □ No
- □ N/A (Cash)

Title Commitment Cleared?

- □ Yes
- □ No

Closing Scheduled?

- □ Yes
- □ No

Is Buyer Performance at Risk?

- □ Yes
- □ No

## TIMELINE RISK REVIEW

Primary Timeline Threat:

---

Does Delay Increase Accrued Loss?

- □ Yes
- □ No

Is File Still Within Viable Window?

- □ Yes
- □ No

Immediate Action Required:

---

# Negotiation Phase Notes

Document strategic observations, negotiation posture adjustments, and risk evolution during active execution.
Record reasoning behind tactical decisions and concessions.

**CURRENT NEGOTIATION POSTURE**

Primary Objective:

---

---

Current Leverage Position:

---

---

Is Position Strengthening or Weakening?

---

**LENDER BEHAVIOR OBSERVATIONS**

Decision Pattern Observed:

---

Internal Approval Signals:

---

Resistance Points:

---

Shift in Tone or Authority Level:

---

**ECONOMIC MOVEMENT ANALYSIS**

Recent Concessions Made:

---

Recent Concessions Requested:

---

Net Direction of Movement:

---

Is Movement Sustainable?

---

**JUNIOR / THIRD-PARTY INFLUENCE**

Impact of Junior Lienholder:

---

Interference or Delay Factors:

---

Coordination Strategy:

---

**TIMELINE PRESSURE ANALYSIS**

Clock Pressure Source:

___

Is Time Increasing Leverage?

___

Risk of Deadline Failure:

___

**STRATEGIC ADJUSTMENT NOTES**

Has Strategy Shifted?

- □ Yes
- □ No

Reason for Shift:

___

___

Next Tactical Move:

___

Fallback Plan if Rejected:

___

**OPERATOR REFLECTION**

Are Decisions Data-Driven or Emotional?

___

Is File Still Within Kill Criteria?

___

Would I Enter This Deal Again Knowing Current Information?

___

# Negotiation Phase Notes

Document strategic observations, negotiation posture adjustments, and risk evolution during active execution.
Record reasoning behind tactical decisions and concessions.

**CURRENT NEGOTIATION POSTURE**

Primary Objective:

______________________________________________

______________________________________________

Current Leverage Position:

______________________________________________

______________________________________________

Is Position Strengthening or Weakening?

______________________________________________

**LENDER BEHAVIOR OBSERVATIONS**

Decision Pattern Observed:

______________________________________________

Internal Approval Signals:

______________________________________________

Resistance Points:

______________________________________________

Shift in Tone or Authority Level:

______________________________________________

**ECONOMIC MOVEMENT ANALYSIS**

Recent Concessions Made:

______________________________________________

Recent Concessions Requested:

______________________________________________

Net Direction of Movement:

______________________________________________

Is Movement Sustainable?

______________________________________________

**JUNIOR / THIRD-PARTY INFLUENCE**

Impact of Junior Lienholder:

______________________________________________

Interference or Delay Factors:

______________________________________________

Coordination Strategy:

______________________________________________

## TIMELINE PRESSURE ANALYSIS

Clock Pressure Source:

______________________________________________

Is Time Increasing Leverage?

______________________________________________

Risk of Deadline Failure:

______________________________________________

## STRATEGIC ADJUSTMENT NOTES

Has Strategy Shifted?

- □ Yes
- □ No

Reason for Shift:

______________________________________________

______________________________________________

Next Tactical Move:

______________________________________________

Fallback Plan if Rejected:

______________________________________________

## OPERATOR REFLECTION

Are Decisions Data-Driven or Emotional?

______________________________________________

Is File Still Within Kill Criteria?

______________________________________________

Would I Enter This Deal Again Knowing Current Information?

______________________________________________

# Negotiation Phase Notes

Document strategic observations, negotiation posture adjustments, and risk evolution during active execution.
Record reasoning behind tactical decisions and concessions.

**CURRENT NEGOTIATION POSTURE**

Primary Objective:

___

___

Current Leverage Position:

___

___

Is Position Strengthening or Weakening?

___

**LENDER BEHAVIOR OBSERVATIONS**

Decision Pattern Observed:

___

Internal Approval Signals:

___

Resistance Points:

___

Shift in Tone or Authority Level:

___

**ECONOMIC MOVEMENT ANALYSIS**

Recent Concessions Made:

___

Recent Concessions Requested:

___

Net Direction of Movement:

___

Is Movement Sustainable?

___

**JUNIOR / THIRD-PARTY INFLUENCE**

Impact of Junior Lienholder:

___

Interference or Delay Factors:

___

Coordination Strategy:

___

## TIMELINE PRESSURE ANALYSIS

Clock Pressure Source:

---

Is Time Increasing Leverage?

---

Risk of Deadline Failure:

---

## STRATEGIC ADJUSTMENT NOTES

Has Strategy Shifted?

- □ Yes
- □ No

Reason for Shift:

---

---

Next Tactical Move:

---

Fallback Plan if Rejected:

---

## OPERATOR REFLECTION

Are Decisions Data-Driven or Emotional?

---

Is File Still Within Kill Criteria?

---

Would I Enter This Deal Again Knowing Current Information?

---

# Negotiation Phase Notes

Document strategic observations, negotiation posture adjustments, and risk evolution during active execution.
Record reasoning behind tactical decisions and concessions.

## CURRENT NEGOTIATION POSTURE

Primary Objective:

______________________________________________

______________________________________________

Current Leverage Position:

______________________________________________

______________________________________________

Is Position Strengthening or Weakening?

______________________________________________

## LENDER BEHAVIOR OBSERVATIONS

Decision Pattern Observed:

______________________________________________

Internal Approval Signals:

______________________________________________

Resistance Points:

______________________________________________

Shift in Tone or Authority Level:

______________________________________________

## ECONOMIC MOVEMENT ANALYSIS

Recent Concessions Made:

______________________________________________

Recent Concessions Requested:

______________________________________________

Net Direction of Movement:

______________________________________________

Is Movement Sustainable?

______________________________________________

## JUNIOR / THIRD-PARTY INFLUENCE

Impact of Junior Lienholder:

______________________________________________

Interference or Delay Factors:

______________________________________________

Coordination Strategy:

______________________________________________

**TIMELINE PRESSURE ANALYSIS**

Clock Pressure Source:

---

Is Time Increasing Leverage?

---

Risk of Deadline Failure:

---

**STRATEGIC ADJUSTMENT NOTES**

Has Strategy Shifted?

- □ Yes
- □ No

Reason for Shift:

---

---

Next Tactical Move:

---

Fallback Plan if Rejected:

---

**OPERATOR REFLECTION**

Are Decisions Data-Driven or Emotional?

---

Is File Still Within Kill Criteria?

---

Would I Enter This Deal Again Knowing Current Information?

---

## Negotiation Phase Notes

Document strategic observations, negotiation posture adjustments, and risk evolution during active execution.
Record reasoning behind tactical decisions and concessions.

### CURRENT NEGOTIATION POSTURE

Primary Objective:

________________________________________

________________________________________

Current Leverage Position:

________________________________________

________________________________________

Is Position Strengthening or Weakening?

________________________________________

### LENDER BEHAVIOR OBSERVATIONS

Decision Pattern Observed:

________________________________________

Internal Approval Signals:

________________________________________

Resistance Points:

________________________________________

Shift in Tone or Authority Level:

________________________________________

### ECONOMIC MOVEMENT ANALYSIS

Recent Concessions Made:

________________________________________

Recent Concessions Requested:

________________________________________

Net Direction of Movement:

________________________________________

Is Movement Sustainable?

________________________________________

### JUNIOR / THIRD-PARTY INFLUENCE

Impact of Junior Lienholder:

________________________________________

Interference or Delay Factors:

________________________________________

Coordination Strategy:

________________________________________

**TIMELINE PRESSURE ANALYSIS**

Clock Pressure Source:

______________________________________________

Is Time Increasing Leverage?

______________________________________________

Risk of Deadline Failure:

______________________________________________

**STRATEGIC ADJUSTMENT NOTES**

Has Strategy Shifted?

□ Yes

□ No

Reason for Shift:

______________________________________________

______________________________________________

Next Tactical Move:

______________________________________________

Fallback Plan if Rejected:

______________________________________________

**OPERATOR REFLECTION**

Are Decisions Data-Driven or Emotional?

______________________________________________

Is File Still Within Kill Criteria?

______________________________________________

Would I Enter This Deal Again Knowing Current Information?

______________________________________________

# Negotiation Phase Notes

Document strategic observations, negotiation posture adjustments, and risk evolution during active execution.
Record reasoning behind tactical decisions and concessions.

**CURRENT NEGOTIATION POSTURE**

Primary Objective:

_______________________________________________

_______________________________________________

Current Leverage Position:

_______________________________________________

_______________________________________________

Is Position Strengthening or Weakening?

_______________________________________________

**LENDER BEHAVIOR OBSERVATIONS**

Decision Pattern Observed:

_______________________________________________

Internal Approval Signals:

_______________________________________________

Resistance Points:

_______________________________________________

Shift in Tone or Authority Level:

_______________________________________________

**ECONOMIC MOVEMENT ANALYSIS**

Recent Concessions Made:

_______________________________________________

Recent Concessions Requested:

_______________________________________________

Net Direction of Movement:

_______________________________________________

Is Movement Sustainable?

_______________________________________________

**JUNIOR / THIRD-PARTY INFLUENCE**

Impact of Junior Lienholder:

_______________________________________________

Interference or Delay Factors:

_______________________________________________

Coordination Strategy:

_______________________________________________

**TIMELINE PRESSURE ANALYSIS**

Clock Pressure Source:

_______________________________________________

Is Time Increasing Leverage?

_______________________________________________

Risk of Deadline Failure:

_______________________________________________

**STRATEGIC ADJUSTMENT NOTES**

Has Strategy Shifted?

- □ Yes
- □ No

Reason for Shift:

_______________________________________________

_______________________________________________

Next Tactical Move:

_______________________________________________

Fallback Plan if Rejected:

_______________________________________________

**OPERATOR REFLECTION**

Are Decisions Data-Driven or Emotional?

_______________________________________________

Is File Still Within Kill Criteria?

_______________________________________________

Would I Enter This Deal Again Knowing Current Information?

_______________________________________________

# Gate III – Structuring Authorization

## Phase III — Structured Notes

Document observations, tactical considerations, or material developments not captured in structured worksheets.
Maintain objective, execution-focused notation.

# PHASE IV
# EXECUTION

(Motivation & Behavioral Risk Evaluation)

# Orientation

**Phase IV controls submission and negotiation mechanics.**

This phase governs:
- Documentation completeness
- Hardship presentation
- Valuation defense
- Lender communication
- Escalation control
- Concession tracking
- Timeline compliance

Execution is disciplined interaction.

Advancement beyond this phase requires structured authorization prior to submission or final approval movement.

***"Discipline Governs Interaction."***

## Seller Motivation Assessment

Evaluate seller motivation, cooperation probability, and behavioral risk factors. Document observable indicators and alignment with transaction objectives.

### DISTRESS DRIVER IDENTIFICATION

Primary Distress Cause:

- □ Income Loss
- □ Business Failure
- □ Vacancy / Cash Flow Collapse
- □ Divorce
- □ Litigation
- □ Health Event
- □ Market Decline
- □ Overleveraging
- □ Other

Is Distress Ongoing or Resolved?

- □ Ongoing
- □ Resolved
- □ Temporary
- □ Unknown

Severity of Distress:

- □ Mild
- □ Moderate
- □ Severe

Notes:

---

### SELLER OBJECTIVE CLARITY

Seller's Stated Objective:

---

Is Objective Realistic?

- □ Yes
- □ No
- □ Uncertain

Is Seller Seeking Full Release of Liability?

- □ Yes
- □ No
- □ Not Addressed

Is Seller Emotionally Anchored to Unrealistic Value?

- □ Yes
- □ No

## COOPERATION INDICATORS

Financial Documents Provided Promptly?

- □ Yes
- □ No

Responsive to Communication?

- □ Yes
- □ No

Willing to Sign Required Disclosures?

- □ Yes
- □ No

Willing to Contribute Cash (If Required)?

- □ Yes
- □ No
- □ Unknown

Appears Transparent Regarding Assets?

- □ Yes
- □ No
- □ Uncertain

## BEHAVIORAL RISK FACTORS

History of Missed Commitments?

- □ Yes
- □ No

Evidence of Withholding Information?

- □ Yes
- □ No

Conflict Between Co-Owners?

- □ Yes
- □ No

Bankruptcy Considered or Threatened?

- □ Yes
- □ No

Risk of Abandonment of Process?

- □ Low
- □ Moderate
- □ High

## WALK-AWAY PROBABILITY ANALYSIS

Would Seller Proceed if Required to Contribute?

- □ Yes
- □ No
- □ Uncertain

Would Seller Proceed if Timeline Extends?

- □ Yes
- □ No
- □ Uncertain

Phase IV
ExecutionWould Seller Proceed if Deficiency Not Fully Waived?

Would Seller Proceed if Deficiency Not Fully Waived?

- □ Yes
- □ No
- □ Uncertain

Estimated Walk-Away Probability:

- □ Low
- □ Moderate
- □ High

**ALIGNMENT WITH STRATEGY**

Is Seller Aligned With Transaction Strategy?

- □ Yes
- □ No
- □ Partially

Does Seller Understand Consequences of Failure?

- □ Yes
- □ No

Is Seller Dependent on Operator for Process Discipline?

- □ Yes
- □ No

**MOTIVATION SCORE (Internal Use)**

Overall Motivation Strength:

- □ Strong
- □ Moderate
- □ Weak

Cooperation Reliability:

- □ Reliable
- □ Unpredictable
- □ High Risk

Proceed to Structuring?

- □ Yes
- □ No
- □ Conditional

Operator Notes:

_______________________________________________

_______________________________________________

# Cooperation Scorecard

Evaluate seller cooperation behavior throughout the transaction lifecycle.
Score objectively based on observed performance, not stated intent.

## COOPERATION METRIC TABLE

| Metric | Observation | Score (1-5) | Evidence | Notes |
|---|---|---|---|---|
| Document Responsiveness | | | | |
| Communication Timeliness | | | | |
| Transparency of Financial Disclosure | | | | |
| Willingness to Follow Process | | | | |
| Realistic Expectation Alignment | | | | |
| Commitment to Closing Timeline | | | | |
| Stability of Participation | | | | |
| Emotional Volatility Impact | | | | |
| Alignment With Operator Strategy | | | | |
| Consistency Under Pressure | | | | |

**Scoring Guidance**

1 = Severely Deficient
2 = Weak
3 = Acceptable
4 = Strong
5 = Exceptional

**SCORE SUMMARY**

Total Score (Sum of Metrics):

___

Average Score:

___

Cooperation Classification:

- □ High Reliability
- □ Moderate Reliability
- □ Elevated Risk
- □ Critical Risk

**TREND ANALYSIS**

Is Cooperation Improving?

- □ Yes
- □ No
- □ Stable

Has Seller Missed Any Commitments?

- □ Yes
- □ No

Number of Missed Commitments:

___

Is Escalation of Structure Required?

- □ Yes
- □ No

**STRATEGIC RESPONSE**

Is Additional Control Required?

- □ Yes
- □ No

Is Backup Plan Necessary?

- □ Yes
- □ No

Should Kill Criteria Be Revisited?

- □ Yes
- □ No

Operator Notes:

___

___

# Behavioral Risk Indicators

Identify observable behaviors that increase execution risk.
Document objective indicators and assess probability of process disruption.

**DOCUMENTATION BEHAVIOR**

Delayed Financial Document Submission?

- □ Yes
- □ No

Repeated Missing Documents?

- □ Yes
- □ No

Inconsistent Financial Disclosures?

- □ Yes
- □ No

Selective Disclosure Suspected?

- □ Yes
- □ No

Evidence:

---

**COMMUNICATION PATTERN**

Unresponsive for > 5 Business Days?

- □ Yes
- □ No

Frequent Change in Narrative?

- □ Yes
- □ No

Avoids Direct Questions?

- □ Yes
- □ No

Escalates Emotionally Under Pressure?

- □ Yes
- □ No

Evidence:

---

**DECISION CONSISTENCY**

Reverses Prior Commitments?

- □ Yes
- □ No

Agrees Verbally but Fails to Act?

- □ Yes
- □ No

Unwilling to Sign Required Forms?

- □ Yes
- □ No

Phase IV
ExecutionAttempts to Circumvent Structured Process?

Attempts to Circumvent Structured Process?

- □ Yes
- □ No

Evidence:

---

**EXTERNAL STRESS FACTORS**

Divorce / Ownership Conflict Active?

- □ Yes
- □ No

Litigation Pending?

- □ Yes
- □ No

Bankruptcy Consultation Confirmed?

- □ Yes
- □ No

Family / Partner Opposition to Sale?

- □ Yes
- □ No

Substance or Mental Health Concerns Observed?

- □ Yes
- □ No
- □ Not Observed

Evidence:

---

**PROCESS DISRUPTION RISK**

Risk of Late-Stage Withdrawal:

- □ Low
- □ Moderate
- □ High

Risk of Bankruptcy Filing:

- □ Low
- □ Moderate
- □ High

Risk of Refusal to Close:

- □ Low
- □ Moderate
- □ High

Risk of Non-Cooperation With Lender Requests:

- □ Low
- □ Moderate
- □ High

## OVERALL BEHAVIORAL RISK CLASSIFICATION

Overall Behavioral Stability:

- □ Stable
- □ Moderately Volatile
- □ High Volatility

Requires Additional Structural Controls?

- □ Yes
- □ No

Should Kill Criteria Be Reviewed?

- □ Yes
- □ No

Operator Notes:

______________________________________________________________________________

______________________________________________________________________________

# Walk-Away Probability Analysis

Evaluate probability of seller withdrawal prior to closing.
Assess behavioral, financial, legal, and emotional triggers objectively.

## FINANCIAL PRESSURE ANALYSIS

Is Seller Currently Making Payments?

- □ Yes
- □ No

Is Seller Experiencing Immediate Cash Crisis?

- □ Yes
- □ No

Is There Asset Equity Outside Subject Property?

- □ Yes
- □ No

Would Seller Benefit From Delay?

- □ Yes
- □ No

Financial Pressure Level:

- □ Low
- □ Moderate
- □ High

## LIABILITY EXPOSURE

Is Loan Recourse?

- □ Yes
- □ No
- □ Unknown

Is Deficiency Release Critical to Seller?

- □ Yes
- □ No

Has Seller Consulted Bankruptcy Counsel?

- □ Yes
- □ No

Is Bankruptcy Filing a Realistic Alternative?

- □ Yes
- □ No

Liability Sensitivity Level:

- □ Low
- □ Moderate
- □ High

## EMOTIONAL & BEHAVIORAL FACTORS

Is Seller Emotionally Attached to Property?

- □ Yes
- □ No

Has Seller Displayed Instability Under Pressure?

□ Yes
□ No

Has Seller Previously Threatened to Abandon Process?

□ Yes
□ No

Does Seller Blame External Parties for Distress?

□ Yes
□ No

Behavioral Withdrawal Risk:

□ Low
□ Moderate
□ High

**PROCESS FATIGUE RISK**

Length of Distress (Months):

___

Is Seller Exhibiting Fatigue?

□ Yes
□ No

Is Seller Expressing Frustration With Timeline?

□ Yes
□ No

Is Seller Losing Confidence in Approval Likelihood?

□ Yes
□ No

Fatigue Risk Level:

□ Low
□ Moderate
□ High

**EXTERNAL DISRUPTION FACTORS**

Divorce or Ownership Conflict Active?

□ Yes
□ No

Pending Litigation?

□ Yes
□ No

Relocation Deadline Approaching?

□ Yes
□ No

Family Opposition to Sale?

□ Yes
□ No

External Disruption Risk:

□ Low
□ Moderate
□ High

## WITHDRAWAL TRIGGER MODEL

Most Likely Withdrawal Trigger:

___

At What Stage Is Seller Most Likely to Walk?

- □ Pre-Submission
- □ Post-BPO
- □ During Negotiation
- □ Pre-Closing
- □ At Approval Conditions

Early Warning Indicators to Monitor:

___

___

## OVERALL WALK-AWAY PROBABILITY

Estimated Walk-Away Probability:

- □ Low (<20%)
- □ Moderate (20–50%)
- □ High (50–75%)
- □ Critical (>75%)

Mitigation Strategy Required?

- □ Yes
- □ No

Kill Criteria Reassessment Required?

- □ Yes
- □ No

Operator Notes:

___

___

# Bankruptcy Risk Review

Assess probability and impact of borrower bankruptcy filing.
Evaluate financial incentive, legal positioning, and timing risk objectively.

**PRIOR BANKRUPTCY HISTORY**

Has Seller Filed Bankruptcy Previously?

- □ Yes
- □ No

Chapter Filed Previously:

- □ 7
- □ 11
- □ 13
- □ Unknown

Date of Prior Filing:

______________________________________________________________________

Was Case Discharged?

- □ Yes
- □ No
- □ Unknown

**CURRENT BANKRUPTCY SIGNALS**

Has Seller Consulted Bankruptcy Counsel?

- □ Yes
- □ No

Has Seller Mentioned Filing?

- □ Yes
- □ No

Is Bankruptcy Being Used as Negotiation Threat?

- □ Yes
- □ No

Is Seller Facing Multiple Creditor Actions?

- □ Yes
- □ No

Current Bankruptcy Signaling Level:

- □ None
- □ Mild
- □ Moderate
- □ Active

**FINANCIAL INCENTIVE ANALYSIS**

Would Bankruptcy Eliminate Personal Liability?

- □ Yes
- □ No
- □ Partial

Would Bankruptcy Improve Seller Position?

- □ Yes

□ No

Would Bankruptcy Delay Foreclosure?

□ Yes

□ No

Is Seller Judgment-Proof Regardless?

□ Yes

□ No

Bankruptcy Economic Incentive Level:

□ Low

□ Moderate

□ High

## STRATEGIC IMPACT ASSESSMENT

If Filed, Would Short Sale Still Proceed?

□ Yes

□ No

□ Uncertain

Would Court Approval Be Required?

□ Yes

□ No

Would Junior Lien Position Change?

□ Yes

□ No

Would Automatic Stay Alter Timeline?

□ Yes

□ No

Impact Severity If Filed:

□ Low

□ Moderate

□ High

□ Deal-Terminating

## TIMING RISK ANALYSIS

Stage of Transaction Most Vulnerable to Filing:

□ Pre-Submission

□ During Negotiation

□ Post-Approval

□ Pre-Closing

Is Seller Under Increasing Legal Pressure?

□ Yes

□ No

Are Garnishments / Judgments Pending?

□ Yes

□ No

Timeline Bankruptcy Risk Level:

□ Low

□ Moderate

Phase IV
Execution□ High

□ High

**MITIGATION STRATEGY**

Has Bankruptcy Risk Been Discussed Directly With Seller?
- □ Yes
- □ No

Is Seller Incentivized to Avoid Filing?
- □ Yes
- □ No

Is Contingency Plan Modeled?
- □ Yes
- □ No

Mitigation Steps Identified:

______________________________________________________________________

______________________________________________________________________

**OVERALL BANKRUPTCY RISK CLASSIFICATION**

Estimated Probability of Filing:
- □ Low (<15%)
- □ Moderate (15–40%)
- □ High (40–70%)
- □ Critical (>70%)

Would Bankruptcy Filing Terminate Deal?
- □ Yes
- □ No
- □ Possibly

Proceed to Structuring?
- □ Yes
- □ Conditional
- □ No

Operator Notes:

______________________________________________________________________

______________________________________________________________________

# Occupancy Risk Evaluation

Assess occupancy status, access control, and possession-related execution risk.
Evaluate impact on valuation, buyer performance, and closing certainty.

## CURRENT OCCUPANCY STATUS

Property Type:

□ Owner-Occupied
□ Tenant-Occupied
□ Mixed Use
□ Vacant

Number of Units (if applicable):

---

Vacancy Rate (if applicable):

---

Is Property Secure?

□ Yes
□ No

## OWNER OCCUPANCY RISK

Is Seller Cooperative With Property Access?

□ Yes
□ No

Is Seller Preparing for Relocation?

□ Yes
□ No

Has Seller Expressed Reluctance to Vacate?

□ Yes
□ No

Is Move-Out Timeline Defined?

□ Yes
□ No

Owner Occupancy Risk Level:

□ Low
□ Moderate
□ High

## TENANT OCCUPANCY RISK

Are Leases Current and Valid?

□ Yes
□ No

Are Tenants in Arrears?

□ Yes
□ No

Are There Active Evictions?

□ Yes
□ No

Are Leases Assignable?

□ Yes
□ No

Are Tenants Cooperative With Showings?

□ Yes
□ No

Tenant Occupancy Risk Level:

□ Low
□ Moderate
□ High

## ACCESS & CONDITION CONTROL

Is Property Accessible for Inspection?

□ Yes
□ No

Is Condition Deteriorating?

□ Yes
□ No

Is Deferred Maintenance Accelerating?

□ Yes
□ No

Is Vandalism Risk Present?

□ Yes
□ No

Condition Control Risk Level:

□ Low
□ Moderate
□ High

## POSSESSION AT CLOSING

Will Property Be Delivered Vacant?

□ Yes
□ No
□ Unknown

Is Post-Closing Possession Requested?

□ Yes
□ No

Is Holdover Risk Present?

□ Yes
□ No

Has Relocation Plan Been Confirmed?

□ Yes
□ No

Possession Risk Level:

□ Low
□ Moderate
□ High

## INSURANCE & LIABILITY EXPOSURE

Is Insurance Current?

□ Yes

□ No

Is Property Insurable in Current Condition?

□ Yes

□ No

Is Liability Exposure Elevated Due to Vacancy?

□ Yes

□ No

Insurance Risk Level:

□ Low

□ Moderate

□ High

## OVERALL OCCUPANCY RISK CLASSIFICATION

Primary Occupancy Threat:

______________________________________________________________________

Does Occupancy Threaten Closing Certainty?

□ Yes

□ No

Mitigation Required?

□ Yes

□ No

Kill Criteria Impacted?

□ Yes

□ No

Operator Notes:

______________________________________________________________________

______________________________________________________________________

# Relocation & Incentive Strategy Planner

Plan seller relocation logistics and incentive alignment to protect closing certainty. Document relocation readiness and structured incentives objectively.

## RELOCATION STATUS

Has Seller Identified Next Residence?

- □ Yes
- □ No

Is Lease Signed for Replacement Housing?

- □ Yes
- □ No

Is Seller Purchasing Replacement Property?

- □ Yes
- □ No

Move-Out Date Identified?

- □ Yes
- □ No

Is Relocation Contingent on Short Sale Proceeds?

- □ Yes
- □ No

Relocation Readiness Level:

- □ Ready
- □ Planning
- □ Unprepared

## FINANCIAL INCENTIVE STRUCTURE

Is Relocation Assistance Available From Lender?

- □ Yes
- □ No
- □ Unknown

Relocation Assistance Amount (If Offered):

________________________________________________________________________

Is Buyer Offering Incentive?

- □ Yes
- □ No

Is Seller Expecting Incentive Beyond Lender Approval?

- □ Yes
- □ No

Is Incentive Structurally Compliant?

- □ Yes
- □ No

## POSSESSION CONTROL PLAN

Will Property Be Vacant at Closing?

- □ Yes
- □ No

Phase IV
ExecutionIs Rent-Back Being Requested?

Is Rent-Back Being Requested?
- □ Yes
- □ No

Is Post-Closing Occupancy Agreement Required?
- □ Yes
- □ No

Holdover Risk Present?
- □ Yes
- □ No

Keys Delivered At:
- □ Closing
- □ Pre-Closing
- □ Other

## EXECUTION ALIGNMENT

Is Seller Financially Dependent on Relocation Funds?
- □ Yes
- □ No

Would Failure to Receive Incentive Cause Withdrawal?
- □ Yes
- □ No

Is Incentive Conditioned on Clean Property Delivery?
- □ Yes
- □ No

Is Property Condition at Risk Due to Move-Out?
- □ Yes
- □ No

## TIMELINE SYNCHRONIZATION

Does Relocation Timeline Align With Closing Date?
- □ Yes
- □ No

Is Seller Under External Relocation Deadline?
- □ Yes
- □ No

Is There Gap Risk Between Approval and Move-Out?
- □ Yes
- □ No

Mitigation Plan:

______________________________________________________________________

______________________________________________________________________

## OVERALL INCENTIVE & RELOCATION RISK

Primary Relocation Risk:

______________________________________________________________________

Probability of Relocation-Driven Delay:

- □ Low
- □ Moderate
- □ High

Does Relocation Strategy Increase Closing Certainty?

- □ Yes
- □ No

Kill Criteria Impacted?

- □ Yes
- □ No

Operator Notes:

_______________________________________________

_______________________________________________

## Seller Interaction Notes

Document material interactions with seller.
Record observable behavior, commitments made, and execution alignment objectively.

### INTERACTION RECORD

Date of Interaction:

---

Method:

- □ Phone
- □ In-Person
- □ Email
- □ Text
- □ Video Conference

Duration:

---

### DISCUSSION SUMMARY

Topics Discussed:

---

---

Seller Concerns Raised:

---

New Information Disclosed:

---

### COMMITMENTS & AGREEMENTS

Documents Promised:

---

Actions Seller Agreed To Take:

---

Deadlines Discussed:

---

Was Commitment Clear and Understood?

- □ Yes
- □ No

### OBSERVABLE BEHAVIOR

Emotional State Observed:

- □ Calm
- □ Anxious
- □ Defensive
- □ Frustrated
- □ Cooperative
- □ Volatile

Consistency With Prior Statements:

- □ Consistent
- □ Inconsistent

Confidence in Process:

- □ High
- □ Moderate
- □ Low

Trust Alignment With Operator:

- □ Strong
- □ Moderate
- □ Weak

**RISK SIGNALS**

Did Seller Express Doubt About Proceeding?

- □ Yes
- □ No

Did Seller Mention Bankruptcy?

- □ Yes
- □ No

Did Seller Reference External Advice Influencing Decision?

- □ Yes
- □ No

Is Withdrawal Risk Increasing?

- □ Yes
- □ No

**STRATEGIC RESPONSE**

Follow-Up Required:

______________________________________________________________________

Additional Structure Required?

- □ Yes
- □ No

Should Cooperation Score Be Updated?

- □ Yes
- □ No

Operator Reflection:

______________________________________________________________________

______________________________________________________________________

# Seller Interaction Notes

Document material interactions with seller.
Record observable behavior, commitments made, and execution alignment objectively.

### INTERACTION RECORD

Date of Interaction:

---

Method:

- □ Phone
- □ In-Person
- □ Email
- □ Text
- □ Video Conference

Duration:

---

### DISCUSSION SUMMARY

Topics Discussed:

---

---

Seller Concerns Raised:

---

New Information Disclosed:

---

### COMMITMENTS & AGREEMENTS

Documents Promised:

---

Actions Seller Agreed To Take:

---

Deadlines Discussed:

---

Was Commitment Clear and Understood?

- □ Yes
- □ No

### OBSERVABLE BEHAVIOR

Emotional State Observed:

- □ Calm
- □ Anxious
- □ Defensive
- □ Frustrated
- □ Cooperative
- □ Volatile

Consistency With Prior Statements:

- □ Consistent
- □ Inconsistent

Confidence in Process:

- □ High
- □ Moderate
- □ Low

Trust Alignment With Operator:

- □ Strong
- □ Moderate
- □ Weak

**RISK SIGNALS**

Did Seller Express Doubt About Proceeding?

- □ Yes
- □ No

Did Seller Mention Bankruptcy?

- □ Yes
- □ No

Did Seller Reference External Advice Influencing Decision?

- □ Yes
- □ No

Is Withdrawal Risk Increasing?

- □ Yes
- □ No

**STRATEGIC RESPONSE**

Follow-Up Required:

_______________________________________________

Additional Structure Required?

- □ Yes
- □ No

Should Cooperation Score Be Updated?

- □ Yes
- □ No

Operator Reflection:

_______________________________________________

_______________________________________________

# Seller Interaction Notes

Document material interactions with seller.
Record observable behavior, commitments made, and execution alignment objectively.

**INTERACTION RECORD**

Date of Interaction:

---

Method:

- □ Phone
- □ In-Person
- □ Email
- □ Text
- □ Video Conference

Duration:

---

**DISCUSSION SUMMARY**

Topics Discussed:

---

---

Seller Concerns Raised:

---

New Information Disclosed:

---

**COMMITMENTS & AGREEMENTS**

Documents Promised:

---

Actions Seller Agreed To Take:

---

Deadlines Discussed:

---

Was Commitment Clear and Understood?

- □ Yes
- □ No

**OBSERVABLE BEHAVIOR**

Emotional State Observed:

- □ Calm
- □ Anxious
- □ Defensive
- □ Frustrated
- □ Cooperative
- □ Volatile

Consistency With Prior Statements:

□ Consistent

□ Inconsistent

Confidence in Process:

□ High

□ Moderate

□ Low

Trust Alignment With Operator:

□ Strong

□ Moderate

□ Weak

**RISK SIGNALS**

Did Seller Express Doubt About Proceeding?

□ Yes

□ No

Did Seller Mention Bankruptcy?

□ Yes

□ No

Did Seller Reference External Advice Influencing Decision?

□ Yes

□ No

Is Withdrawal Risk Increasing?

□ Yes

□ No

**STRATEGIC RESPONSE**

Follow-Up Required:

___

Additional Structure Required?

□ Yes

□ No

Should Cooperation Score Be Updated?

□ Yes

□ No

Operator Reflection:

___

___

# Seller Interaction Notes

Document material interactions with seller.
Record observable behavior, commitments made, and execution alignment objectively.

**INTERACTION RECORD**

Date of Interaction:

---

Method:

- □ Phone
- □ In-Person
- □ Email
- □ Text
- □ Video Conference

Duration:

---

**DISCUSSION SUMMARY**

Topics Discussed:

---

---

Seller Concerns Raised:

---

New Information Disclosed:

---

**COMMITMENTS & AGREEMENTS**

Documents Promised:

---

Actions Seller Agreed To Take:

---

Deadlines Discussed:

---

Was Commitment Clear and Understood?

- □ Yes
- □ No

**OBSERVABLE BEHAVIOR**

Emotional State Observed:

- □ Calm
- □ Anxious
- □ Defensive
- □ Frustrated
- □ Cooperative
- □ Volatile

Consistency With Prior Statements:

- □ Consistent
- □ Inconsistent

Confidence in Process:

- □ High
- □ Moderate
- □ Low

Trust Alignment With Operator:

- □ Strong
- □ Moderate
- □ Weak

**RISK SIGNALS**

Did Seller Express Doubt About Proceeding?

- □ Yes
- □ No

Did Seller Mention Bankruptcy?

- □ Yes
- □ No

Did Seller Reference External Advice Influencing Decision?

- □ Yes
- □ No

Is Withdrawal Risk Increasing?

- □ Yes
- □ No

**STRATEGIC RESPONSE**

Follow-Up Required:

____________________________________________________________

Additional Structure Required?

- □ Yes
- □ No

Should Cooperation Score Be Updated?

- □ Yes
- □ No

Operator Reflection:

____________________________________________________________

____________________________________________________________

## Seller Interaction Notes

Document material interactions with seller.
Record observable behavior, commitments made, and execution alignment objectively.

**INTERACTION RECORD**

Date of Interaction:

______________________________

Method:

- □ Phone
- □ In-Person
- □ Email
- □ Text
- □ Video Conference

Duration:

______________________________

**DISCUSSION SUMMARY**

Topics Discussed:

______________________________

______________________________

Seller Concerns Raised:

______________________________

New Information Disclosed:

______________________________

**COMMITMENTS & AGREEMENTS**

Documents Promised:

______________________________

Actions Seller Agreed To Take:

______________________________

Deadlines Discussed:

______________________________

Was Commitment Clear and Understood?

- □ Yes
- □ No

**OBSERVABLE BEHAVIOR**

Emotional State Observed:

- □ Calm
- □ Anxious
- □ Defensive
- □ Frustrated
- □ Cooperative
- □ Volatile

Consistency With Prior Statements:

- □ Consistent
- □ Inconsistent

Confidence in Process:

- □ High
- □ Moderate
- □ Low

Trust Alignment With Operator:

- □ Strong
- □ Moderate
- □ Weak

**RISK SIGNALS**

Did Seller Express Doubt About Proceeding?

- □ Yes
- □ No

Did Seller Mention Bankruptcy?

- □ Yes
- □ No

Did Seller Reference External Advice Influencing Decision?

- □ Yes
- □ No

Is Withdrawal Risk Increasing?

- □ Yes
- □ No

**STRATEGIC RESPONSE**

Follow-Up Required:

______________________________________________________________________

Additional Structure Required?

- □ Yes
- □ No

Should Cooperation Score Be Updated?

- □ Yes
- □ No

Operator Reflection:

______________________________________________________________________

______________________________________________________________________

# Seller Interaction Notes

Document material interactions with seller.
Record observable behavior, commitments made, and execution alignment objectively.

## INTERACTION RECORD

Date of Interaction:

---

Method:

- □ Phone
- □ In-Person
- □ Email
- □ Text
- □ Video Conference

Duration:

---

## DISCUSSION SUMMARY

Topics Discussed:

---

---

Seller Concerns Raised:

---

New Information Disclosed:

---

## COMMITMENTS & AGREEMENTS

Documents Promised:

---

Actions Seller Agreed To Take:

---

Deadlines Discussed:

---

Was Commitment Clear and Understood?

- □ Yes
- □ No

## OBSERVABLE BEHAVIOR

Emotional State Observed:

- □ Calm
- □ Anxious
- □ Defensive
- □ Frustrated
- □ Cooperative
- □ Volatile

Consistency With Prior Statements:

- □ Consistent
- □ Inconsistent

Confidence in Process:

- □ High
- □ Moderate
- □ Low

Trust Alignment With Operator:

- □ Strong
- □ Moderate
- □ Weak

**RISK SIGNALS**

Did Seller Express Doubt About Proceeding?

- □ Yes
- □ No

Did Seller Mention Bankruptcy?

- □ Yes
- □ No

Did Seller Reference External Advice Influencing Decision?

- □ Yes
- □ No

Is Withdrawal Risk Increasing?

- □ Yes
- □ No

**STRATEGIC RESPONSE**

Follow-Up Required:

______________________________________________________________________

Additional Structure Required?

- □ Yes
- □ No

Should Cooperation Score Be Updated?

- □ Yes
- □ No

Operator Reflection:

______________________________________________________________________

______________________________________________________________________

# Gate IV – Capital Deployment Authorization

## PRE-SUBMISSION ADVANCEMENT AUTHORIZATION

Submission to lender or loss mitigation is authorized only when the transaction file is complete, valuation support is documented, and negotiation posture is structurally prepared.
If material deficiencies exist, they must be recorded prior to submission.

## SUBMISSION PACKAGE CONFIRMATION

Confirm the following:

- □ Hardship Narrative Completed (if applicable)
- □ Borrower Financial Documentation Verified
- □ Required Supporting Documents Compiled
- □ Comparable Sales Log Updated
- □ Valuation Position Supported
- □ Junior Lien Strategy Defined
- □ Offer Structuring Matrix Finalized
- □ Counteroffer Boundaries Established
- □ Timeline & Foreclosure Exposure Reviewed
- □ Kill Criteria Reconfirmed

## LEVERAGE & POSITION REVIEW

Is Initial Offer Strategically Positioned?

- □ Yes
- □ No

Are Concession Limits Defined?

- □ Yes
- □ No

Is Junior Lien Strategy Predefined?

- □ Yes
- □ No

Is Escalation Strategy Identified?

- □ Yes
- □ No

Is Foreclosure Timeline Controlled or Monitored?

- □ Yes
- □ No

## RISK DISCLOSURE PRIOR TO SUBMISSION

Are There Known Weaknesses in the File?

- □ Yes
- □ No

If Yes, Document:

______________________________________________________________________

______________________________________________________________________

Is Submission Premature?

- □ Yes

□ No

## DEFICIENCIES / CONDITIONAL ADVANCEMENT NOTES

If submission is conditional, document required corrective actions.

____________________________________________________________

____________________________________________________________

____________________________________________________________

## ADVANCEMENT STATUS

- ☐ Authorized — Submit File
- ☐ Authorized with Conditions
- ☐ Defer Submission
- ☐ Do Not Submit

If Defer or Do Not Submit, document rationale:

____________________________________________________________

____________________________________________________________

## AUTHORIZED SIGNATORY

Name: ______________________________

Title / Role: __________________________

Signature: ____________________________

Date: ________________________________

Authority Basis (if applicable):

- ☐ Sole Operator
- ☐ Managing Member
- ☐ General Partner
- ☐ Investment Committee
- ☐ Other

## Phase IV — Structured Notes

Document observations, tactical considerations, or material developments not captured in structured worksheets.
Maintain objective, execution-focused notation.

# PHASE V
# CONTROL & VERIFICATION

# Orientation

**Phase V governs closing authorization and capital deployment.**

This phase confirms:

- Final net position
- Approval compliance
- Lien resolution
- Legal exposure
- Funding confirmation
- Behavioral stability

This phase protects capital.

Completion of this phase requires **Closing Authorization** by an **Authorized Signatory**, documenting formal risk assumption and approval to deploy capital.

***"Authorization Precedes Capital."***

# Task Completion Log

Record all material execution tasks required to advance the file to closing.
Track responsibility, status, and completion verification.

**MASTER TASK TRACKING TABLE**

| Task ID | Task Description | Responsible Party | Related Phase | Date Assigned | Due Date | Status | Completion Date | Notes |
|---|---|---|---|---|---|---|---|---|
| | | | | | | | | |
| | | | | | | | | |
| | | | | | | | | |
| | | | | | | | | |
| | | | | | | | | |
| | | | | | | | | |
| | | | | | | | | |
| | | | | | | | | |
| | | | | | | | | |
| | | | | | | | | |
| | | | | | | | | |
| | | | | | | | | |
| | | | | | | | | |
| | | | | | | | | |
| | | | | | | | | |

**Column Definitions**

**Task ID**

→ Simple reference (e.g., T-01, T-02)

**Task Description**

→ Specific action (e.g., "Obtain Updated Bank Statements")

**Responsible Party**

→ Buyer / Seller / Senior Lender / Junior Lender / Title / Operator

**Related Phase**

→ Phase II / III / IV / V

**Date Assigned**

→ Calendar date

**Due Date**

→ Deadline

**Status**

→ Pending / In Progress / Complete / Delayed / At Risk

**Completion Date**

→ When fully satisfied

**Notes**

→ Brief clarification

**CONDITION-SPECIFIC TRACKING**

Are There Approval Letter Conditions Outstanding?

□ Yes

□ No

Are There Title Cure Items Outstanding?

□ Yes

□ No

Are There Junior Consent Conditions Outstanding?

□ Yes

□ No

Are Buyer Financing Conditions Outstanding?

□ Yes

□ No

Details:

---

**EXECUTION RISK REVIEW**

Any Task Currently At Risk?

□ Yes

□ No

If Yes, Identify:

---

Is Closing Date Threatened?

□ Yes

□ No

Phase V
Control & VerificationDoes Delay Increase Accrued Loss?

Does Delay Increase Accrued Loss?

- □ Yes
- □ No

**ACCOUNTABILITY CONFIRMATION**

Are All Tasks Assigned Clearly?

- □ Yes
- □ No

Is Responsibility Ambiguous Anywhere?

- □ Yes
- □ No

Is Weekly Review Occurring?

- □ Yes
- □ No

Operator Initials:

___

Date:

___

# Task Completion Log

Record all material execution tasks required to advance the file to closing.
Track responsibility, status, and completion verification.

**MASTER TASK TRACKING TABLE**

| Task ID | Task Description | Responsible Party | Related Phase | Date Assigned | Due Date | Status | Completion Date | Notes |
|---|---|---|---|---|---|---|---|---|
| | | | | | | | | |
| | | | | | | | | |
| | | | | | | | | |
| | | | | | | | | |
| | | | | | | | | |
| | | | | | | | | |
| | | | | | | | | |
| | | | | | | | | |
| | | | | | | | | |
| | | | | | | | | |
| | | | | | | | | |
| | | | | | | | | |
| | | | | | | | | |
| | | | | | | | | |
| | | | | | | | | |

**Column Definitions**

**Task ID**
→ Simple reference (e.g., T-01, T-02)

**Task Description**
→ Specific action (e.g., "Obtain Updated Bank Statements")

**Responsible Party**
→ Buyer / Seller / Senior Lender / Junior Lender / Title / Operator

**Related Phase**
→ Phase II / III / IV / V

**Date Assigned**
→ Calendar date

**Due Date**
→ Deadline

**Status**
→ Pending / In Progress / Complete / Delayed / At Risk

**Completion Date**
→ When fully satisfied

**Notes**
→ Brief clarification

**CONDITION-SPECIFIC TRACKING**

Are There Approval Letter Conditions Outstanding?
□ Yes
□ No

Are There Title Cure Items Outstanding?
□ Yes
□ No

Are There Junior Consent Conditions Outstanding?
□ Yes
□ No

Are Buyer Financing Conditions Outstanding?
□ Yes
□ No

Details:

---

**EXECUTION RISK REVIEW**

Any Task Currently At Risk?
□ Yes
□ No

If Yes, Identify:

---

Is Closing Date Threatened?
□ Yes
□ No

Phase V
Control & VerificationDoes Delay Increase Accrued Loss?

Does Delay Increase Accrued Loss?

- □ Yes
- □ No

**ACCOUNTABILITY CONFIRMATION**

Are All Tasks Assigned Clearly?

- □ Yes
- □ No

Is Responsibility Ambiguous Anywhere?

- □ Yes
- □ No

Is Weekly Review Occurring?

- □ Yes
- □ No

Operator Initials:

______________________________________________________________________

Date:

______________________________________________________________________

# Task Completion Log

Record all material execution tasks required to advance the file to closing.
Track responsibility, status, and completion verification.

## MASTER TASK TRACKING TABLE

| Task ID | Task Description | Responsible Party | Related Phase | Date Assigned | Due Date | Status | Completion Date | Notes |
|---|---|---|---|---|---|---|---|---|
| | | | | | | | | |
| | | | | | | | | |
| | | | | | | | | |
| | | | | | | | | |
| | | | | | | | | |
| | | | | | | | | |
| | | | | | | | | |
| | | | | | | | | |
| | | | | | | | | |
| | | | | | | | | |
| | | | | | | | | |
| | | | | | | | | |
| | | | | | | | | |
| | | | | | | | | |
| | | | | | | | | |

**Column Definitions**

**Task ID**

→ Simple reference (e.g., T-01, T-02)

**Task Description**

→ Specific action (e.g., "Obtain Updated Bank Statements")

**Responsible Party**

→ Buyer / Seller / Senior Lender / Junior Lender / Title / Operator

**Related Phase**

→ Phase II / III / IV / V

**Date Assigned**

→ Calendar date

**Due Date**

→ Deadline

**Status**

→ Pending / In Progress / Complete / Delayed / At Risk

**Completion Date**

→ When fully satisfied

**Notes**

→ Brief clarification

**CONDITION-SPECIFIC TRACKING**

Are There Approval Letter Conditions Outstanding?

□ Yes

□ No

Are There Title Cure Items Outstanding?

□ Yes

□ No

Are There Junior Consent Conditions Outstanding?

□ Yes

□ No

Are Buyer Financing Conditions Outstanding?

□ Yes

□ No

Details:

---

**EXECUTION RISK REVIEW**

Any Task Currently At Risk?

□ Yes

□ No

If Yes, Identify:

---

Is Closing Date Threatened?

□ Yes

□ No

Phase V
Control & VerificationDoes Delay Increase Accrued Loss?

Does Delay Increase Accrued Loss?

- □ Yes
- □ No

**ACCOUNTABILITY CONFIRMATION**

Are All Tasks Assigned Clearly?

- □ Yes
- □ No

Is Responsibility Ambiguous Anywhere?

- □ Yes
- □ No

Is Weekly Review Occurring?

- □ Yes
- □ No

Operator Initials:

___

Date:

___

# Task Completion Log

Record all material execution tasks required to advance the file to closing.
Track responsibility, status, and completion verification.

**MASTER TASK TRACKING TABLE**

| Task ID | Task Description | Responsible Party | Related Phase | Date Assigned | Due Date | Status | Completion Date | Notes |
|---|---|---|---|---|---|---|---|---|
| | | | | | | | | |
| | | | | | | | | |
| | | | | | | | | |
| | | | | | | | | |
| | | | | | | | | |
| | | | | | | | | |
| | | | | | | | | |
| | | | | | | | | |
| | | | | | | | | |
| | | | | | | | | |
| | | | | | | | | |
| | | | | | | | | |
| | | | | | | | | |
| | | | | | | | | |
| | | | | | | | | |

**Column Definitions**

**Task ID**

→ Simple reference (e.g., T-01, T-02)

**Task Description**

→ Specific action (e.g., "Obtain Updated Bank Statements")

**Responsible Party**

→ Buyer / Seller / Senior Lender / Junior Lender / Title / Operator

**Related Phase**

→ Phase II / III / IV / V

**Date Assigned**

→ Calendar date

**Due Date**

→ Deadline

**Status**

→ Pending / In Progress / Complete / Delayed / At Risk

**Completion Date**

→ When fully satisfied

**Notes**

→ Brief clarification

## CONDITION-SPECIFIC TRACKING

Are There Approval Letter Conditions Outstanding?

□ Yes

□ No

Are There Title Cure Items Outstanding?

□ Yes

□ No

Are There Junior Consent Conditions Outstanding?

□ Yes

□ No

Are Buyer Financing Conditions Outstanding?

□ Yes

□ No

Details:

---

## EXECUTION RISK REVIEW

Any Task Currently At Risk?

□ Yes

□ No

If Yes, Identify:

---

Is Closing Date Threatened?

□ Yes

□ No

Phase V
Control & VerificationDoes Delay Increase Accrued Loss?

Does Delay Increase Accrued Loss?

- □ Yes
- □ No

**ACCOUNTABILITY CONFIRMATION**

Are All Tasks Assigned Clearly?

- □ Yes
- □ No

Is Responsibility Ambiguous Anywhere?

- □ Yes
- □ No

Is Weekly Review Occurring?

- □ Yes
- □ No

Operator Initials:

______________________________________________________________________

Date:

______________________________________________________________________

# Task Completion Log

Record all material execution tasks required to advance the file to closing.
Track responsibility, status, and completion verification.

**MASTER TASK TRACKING TABLE**

| Task ID | Task Description | Responsible Party | Related Phase | Date Assigned | Due Date | Status | Completion Date | Notes |
|---|---|---|---|---|---|---|---|---|
| | | | | | | | | |
| | | | | | | | | |
| | | | | | | | | |
| | | | | | | | | |
| | | | | | | | | |
| | | | | | | | | |
| | | | | | | | | |
| | | | | | | | | |
| | | | | | | | | |
| | | | | | | | | |
| | | | | | | | | |
| | | | | | | | | |
| | | | | | | | | |
| | | | | | | | | |
| | | | | | | | | |

**Column Definitions**

**Task ID**
→ Simple reference (e.g., T-01, T-02)

**Task Description**
→ Specific action (e.g., "Obtain Updated Bank Statements")

**Responsible Party**
→ Buyer / Seller / Senior Lender / Junior Lender / Title / Operator

**Related Phase**
→ Phase II / III / IV / V

**Date Assigned**
→ Calendar date

**Due Date**
→ Deadline

**Status**
→ Pending / In Progress / Complete / Delayed / At Risk

**Completion Date**
→ When fully satisfied

**Notes**
→ Brief clarification

**CONDITION-SPECIFIC TRACKING**

Are There Approval Letter Conditions Outstanding?
□ Yes
□ No

Are There Title Cure Items Outstanding?
□ Yes
□ No

Are There Junior Consent Conditions Outstanding?
□ Yes
□ No

Are Buyer Financing Conditions Outstanding?
□ Yes
□ No

Details:

---

**EXECUTION RISK REVIEW**

Any Task Currently At Risk?
□ Yes
□ No

If Yes, Identify:

---

Is Closing Date Threatened?
□ Yes
□ No

Phase V
Control & VerificationDoes Delay Increase Accrued Loss?

Does Delay Increase Accrued Loss?

- □ Yes
- □ No

**ACCOUNTABILITY CONFIRMATION**

Are All Tasks Assigned Clearly?

- □ Yes
- □ No

Is Responsibility Ambiguous Anywhere?

- □ Yes
- □ No

Is Weekly Review Occurring?

- □ Yes
- □ No

Operator Initials:

______________________________________________

Date:

______________________________________________

# Decision Log & Rationale Tracker

Document material decisions affecting economic structure, risk allocation, or strategic direction. Record rationale, supporting data, and impact assessment.

**DECISION LOG TABLE**

| Decision ID | Date | Decision Description | Trigger Event | Alternatives Considered | Rationale | Economic Impact | Risk Impact | Approved By | Status |
|---|---|---|---|---|---|---|---|---|---|
| | | | | | | | | | |
| | | | | | | | | | |
| | | | | | | | | | |
| | | | | | | | | | |
| | | | | | | | | | |
| | | | | | | | | | |
| | | | | | | | | | |
| | | | | | | | | | |
| | | | | | | | | | |
| | | | | | | | | | |
| | | | | | | | | | |
| | | | | | | | | | |
| | | | | | | | | | |
| | | | | | | | | | |
| | | | | | | | | | |

**Column Definitions**

**Decision ID**

→ D-01, D-02, etc.

**Date**

→ Calendar date

**Decision Description**

→ Specific action (e.g., "Accepted $15K Buyer Contribution Increase")

**Trigger Event**

→ BPO Revision / Junior Demand / Timeline Pressure / Bankruptcy Threat / Etc.

**Alternatives Considered**

→ Brief summary of rejected options

**Rationale**

→ Objective reasoning

**Economic Impact**

→ Increase / Decrease / Neutral + brief note

**Risk Impact**

→ Reduced / Increased / Neutral

**Approved By**

→ Operator / Investment Committee / Buyer / Etc.

**Status**

→ Active / Reversed / Superseded

**DECISION DRIFT REVIEW**

Has Strategy Shifted From Original Model?

□ Yes

□ No

If Yes, Why:

---

Are Decisions Still Within Kill Criteria?

□ Yes

□ No

Has Economic Profile Deteriorated?

□ Yes

□ No

**HINDSIGHT PROTECTION**

Was Decision Data-Driven?

□ Yes

□ No

Was Decision Time-Pressured?

□ Yes

□ No

Would This Decision Be Made Again Under Same Conditions?

□ Yes

□ No

Lessons Identified:

________________________________________

________________________________________

## CONTROL CONFIRMATION

Are All Material Decisions Logged?

- ☐ Yes
- ☐ No

Is Committee-Level Approval Required for Any Open Decisions?

- ☐ Yes
- ☐ No

Operator Initials:

________________________________________

Date:

________________________________________

# Decision Log & Rationale Tracker

Document material decisions affecting economic structure, risk allocation, or strategic direction. Record rationale, supporting data, and impact assessment.

**DECISION LOG TABLE**

| Decision ID | Date | Decision Description | Trigger Event | Alternatives Considered | Rationale | Economic Impact | Risk Impact | Approved By | Status |
|---|---|---|---|---|---|---|---|---|---|
| | | | | | | | | | |
| | | | | | | | | | |
| | | | | | | | | | |
| | | | | | | | | | |
| | | | | | | | | | |
| | | | | | | | | | |
| | | | | | | | | | |
| | | | | | | | | | |
| | | | | | | | | | |
| | | | | | | | | | |
| | | | | | | | | | |
| | | | | | | | | | |
| | | | | | | | | | |
| | | | | | | | | | |
| | | | | | | | | | |

**Column Definitions**

**Decision ID**
→ D-01, D-02, etc.

**Date**
→ Calendar date

**Decision Description**
→ Specific action (e.g., "Accepted $15K Buyer Contribution Increase")

**Trigger Event**
→ BPO Revision / Junior Demand / Timeline Pressure / Bankruptcy Threat / Etc.

**Alternatives Considered**
→ Brief summary of rejected options

**Rationale**
→ Objective reasoning

**Economic Impact**
→ Increase / Decrease / Neutral + brief note

**Risk Impact**
→ Reduced / Increased / Neutral

**Approved By**
→ Operator / Investment Committee / Buyer / Etc.

**Status**
→ Active / Reversed / Superseded

## DECISION DRIFT REVIEW

Has Strategy Shifted From Original Model?
□ Yes
□ No

If Yes, Why:

---

Are Decisions Still Within Kill Criteria?
□ Yes
□ No

Has Economic Profile Deteriorated?
□ Yes
□ No

## HINDSIGHT PROTECTION

Was Decision Data-Driven?
□ Yes
□ No

Was Decision Time-Pressured?
□ Yes
□ No

Would This Decision Be Made Again Under Same Conditions?
□ Yes
□ No

Lessons Identified:

________________________________________

________________________________________

## CONTROL CONFIRMATION

Are All Material Decisions Logged?

- □ Yes
- □ No

Is Committee-Level Approval Required for Any Open Decisions?

- □ Yes
- □ No

Operator Initials:

________________________________________

Date:

________________________________________

# Decision Log & Rationale Tracker

Document material decisions affecting economic structure, risk allocation, or strategic direction. Record rationale, supporting data, and impact assessment.

### DECISION LOG TABLE

| Decision ID | Date | Decision Description | Trigger Event | Alternatives Considered | Rationale | Economic Impact | Risk Impact | Approved By | Status |
|---|---|---|---|---|---|---|---|---|---|
| | | | | | | | | | |
| | | | | | | | | | |
| | | | | | | | | | |
| | | | | | | | | | |
| | | | | | | | | | |
| | | | | | | | | | |
| | | | | | | | | | |
| | | | | | | | | | |
| | | | | | | | | | |
| | | | | | | | | | |
| | | | | | | | | | |
| | | | | | | | | | |
| | | | | | | | | | |
| | | | | | | | | | |
| | | | | | | | | | |

**Column Definitions**

**Decision ID**

→ D-01, D-02, etc.

**Date**

→ Calendar date

**Decision Description**

→ Specific action (e.g., "Accepted $15K Buyer Contribution Increase")

**Trigger Event**

→ BPO Revision / Junior Demand / Timeline Pressure / Bankruptcy Threat / Etc.

**Alternatives Considered**

→ Brief summary of rejected options

**Rationale**

→ Objective reasoning

**Economic Impact**

→ Increase / Decrease / Neutral + brief note

**Risk Impact**

→ Reduced / Increased / Neutral

**Approved By**

→ Operator / Investment Committee / Buyer / Etc.

**Status**

→ Active / Reversed / Superseded

## DECISION DRIFT REVIEW

Has Strategy Shifted From Original Model?

□ Yes

□ No

If Yes, Why:

______________________________________________________________________

Are Decisions Still Within Kill Criteria?

□ Yes

□ No

Has Economic Profile Deteriorated?

□ Yes

□ No

## HINDSIGHT PROTECTION

Was Decision Data-Driven?

□ Yes

□ No

Was Decision Time-Pressured?

□ Yes

□ No

Would This Decision Be Made Again Under Same Conditions?

□ Yes

□ No

Lessons Identified:

---

---

## CONTROL CONFIRMATION

Are All Material Decisions Logged?

- □ Yes
- □ No

Is Committee-Level Approval Required for Any Open Decisions?

- □ Yes
- □ No

Operator Initials:

---

Date:

---

# Decision Log & Rationale Tracker

Document material decisions affecting economic structure, risk allocation, or strategic direction. Record rationale, supporting data, and impact assessment.

**DECISION LOG TABLE**

| Decision ID | Date | Decision Description | Trigger Event | Alternatives Considered | Rationale | Economic Impact | Risk Impact | Approved By | Status |
|---|---|---|---|---|---|---|---|---|---|
| | | | | | | | | | |
| | | | | | | | | | |
| | | | | | | | | | |
| | | | | | | | | | |
| | | | | | | | | | |
| | | | | | | | | | |
| | | | | | | | | | |
| | | | | | | | | | |
| | | | | | | | | | |
| | | | | | | | | | |
| | | | | | | | | | |
| | | | | | | | | | |
| | | | | | | | | | |
| | | | | | | | | | |
| | | | | | | | | | |

**Column Definitions**

**Decision ID**

→ D-01, D-02, etc.

**Date**

→ Calendar date

**Decision Description**

→ Specific action (e.g., "Accepted $15K Buyer Contribution Increase")

**Trigger Event**

→ BPO Revision / Junior Demand / Timeline Pressure / Bankruptcy Threat / Etc.

**Alternatives Considered**

→ Brief summary of rejected options

**Rationale**

→ Objective reasoning

**Economic Impact**

→ Increase / Decrease / Neutral + brief note

**Risk Impact**

→ Reduced / Increased / Neutral

**Approved By**

→ Operator / Investment Committee / Buyer / Etc.

**Status**

→ Active / Reversed / Superseded

**DECISION DRIFT REVIEW**

Has Strategy Shifted From Original Model?

□ Yes

□ No

If Yes, Why:

______________________________________________________________________

Are Decisions Still Within Kill Criteria?

□ Yes

□ No

Has Economic Profile Deteriorated?

□ Yes

□ No

**HINDSIGHT PROTECTION**

Was Decision Data-Driven?

□ Yes

□ No

Was Decision Time-Pressured?

□ Yes

□ No

Would This Decision Be Made Again Under Same Conditions?

□ Yes

□ No

Lessons Identified:

______________________________________________

______________________________________________

## CONTROL CONFIRMATION

Are All Material Decisions Logged?

- □ Yes
- □ No

Is Committee-Level Approval Required for Any Open Decisions?

- □ Yes
- □ No

Operator Initials:

______________________________________________

Date:

______________________________________________

# Decision Log & Rationale Tracker

Document material decisions affecting economic structure, risk allocation, or strategic direction. Record rationale, supporting data, and impact assessment.

**DECISION LOG TABLE**

| Decision ID | Date | Decision Description | Trigger Event | Alternatives Considered | Rationale | Economic Impact | Risk Impact | Approved By | Status |
|---|---|---|---|---|---|---|---|---|---|
| | | | | | | | | | |
| | | | | | | | | | |
| | | | | | | | | | |
| | | | | | | | | | |
| | | | | | | | | | |
| | | | | | | | | | |
| | | | | | | | | | |
| | | | | | | | | | |
| | | | | | | | | | |
| | | | | | | | | | |
| | | | | | | | | | |
| | | | | | | | | | |
| | | | | | | | | | |
| | | | | | | | | | |
| | | | | | | | | | |

**Column Definitions**

**Decision ID**
→ D-01, D-02, etc.

**Date**
→ Calendar date

**Decision Description**
→ Specific action (e.g., "Accepted $15K Buyer Contribution Increase")

**Trigger Event**
→ BPO Revision / Junior Demand / Timeline Pressure / Bankruptcy Threat / Etc.

**Alternatives Considered**
→ Brief summary of rejected options

**Rationale**
→ Objective reasoning

**Economic Impact**
→ Increase / Decrease / Neutral + brief note

**Risk Impact**
→ Reduced / Increased / Neutral

**Approved By**
→ Operator / Investment Committee / Buyer / Etc.

**Status**
→ Active / Reversed / Superseded

## DECISION DRIFT REVIEW

Has Strategy Shifted From Original Model?
- □ Yes
- □ No

If Yes, Why:

______________________________________________________________________

Are Decisions Still Within Kill Criteria?
- □ Yes
- □ No

Has Economic Profile Deteriorated?
- □ Yes
- □ No

## HINDSIGHT PROTECTION

Was Decision Data-Driven?
- □ Yes
- □ No

Was Decision Time-Pressured?
- □ Yes
- □ No

Would This Decision Be Made Again Under Same Conditions?
- □ Yes
- □ No

Lessons Identified:

___

___

## CONTROL CONFIRMATION

Are All Material Decisions Logged?

- □ Yes
- □ No

Is Committee-Level Approval Required for Any Open Decisions?

- □ Yes
- □ No

Operator Initials:

___

Date:

___

# Concession & Adjustment Record

Record all material economic concessions and structural adjustments.
Track cumulative impact on net position and risk exposure.

**BASELINE ECONOMIC MODEL**

Original Offer Price:

______________________________

Original Net-to-Lender Estimate:

______________________________

Original Buyer Cash Requirement:

______________________________

Original Seller Contribution:

______________________________

Original Closing Timeline:

______________________________

**CONCESSION & ADJUSTMENT TABLE**

| Date | Party Benefiting | Adjustment Type | Description | Amount Impact | Cumulative Impact | Trigger | Approved By | Status |
|---|---|---|---|---|---|---|---|---|
| | | | | | | | | |
| | | | | | | | | |
| | | | | | | | | |
| | | | | | | | | |
| | | | | | | | | |
| | | | | | | | | |
| | | | | | | | | |
| | | | | | | | | |
| | | | | | | | | |
| | | | | | | | | |

| Date | Party Benefiting | Adjustment Type | Description | Amount Impact | Cumulative Impact | Trigger | Approved By | Status |
|---|---|---|---|---|---|---|---|---|
| | | | | | | | | |
| | | | | | | | | |
| | | | | | | | | |
| | | | | | | | | |
| | | | | | | | | |

**Column Definitions**

**Date**

→ Calendar date

**Party Benefiting**

→ Senior Lender / Junior Lender / Buyer / Seller

**Adjustment Type**

→ Price Reduction / Cash Contribution Increase / Repair Credit / Timeline Extension / Fee Waiver / Condition Modification

**Description**

→ Brief factual summary

**Amount Impact**

→ Dollar amount change (increase or decrease)

**Cumulative Impact**

→ Running total of economic drift

**Trigger**

→ BPO / Junior Demand / Timeline Pressure / Committee Condition

**Approved By**

→ Operator / Committee / Buyer

**Status**

→ Active / Reversed / Superseded

**CUMULATIVE IMPACT SUMMARY**

Total Price Adjustments:

___

Total Buyer Concessions:

___

Total Seller Concessions:

___

Total Lender Concessions:

___

Net Drift From Original Structure:

___

## ECONOMIC CONTROL CHECK

Has Deal Drifted Outside Target IRR / Return Model?

□ Yes

□ No

Has Net-to-Lender Improved or Deteriorated?

□ Improved

□ Deteriorated

□ Neutral

Is Economic Profile Still Acceptable?

□ Yes

□ No

Should Kill Criteria Be Revisited?

□ Yes

□ No

## STRATEGIC OBSERVATION

Is Concession Pattern One-Sided?

□ Yes

□ No

Is Leverage Increasing or Decreasing?

□ Increasing

□ Decreasing

□ Stable

Primary Economic Risk Remaining:

______________________________________________________________

Operator Notes:

______________________________________________________________

______________________________________________________________

______________________________________________________________

# Concession & Adjustment Record

Record all material economic concessions and structural adjustments.
Track cumulative impact on net position and risk exposure.

**BASELINE ECONOMIC MODEL**

Original Offer Price:

---

Original Net-to-Lender Estimate:

---

Original Buyer Cash Requirement:

---

Original Seller Contribution:

---

Original Closing Timeline:

---

**CONCESSION & ADJUSTMENT TABLE**

| Date | Party Benefiting | Adjustment Type | Description | Amount Impact | Cumulative Impact | Trigger | Approved By | Status |
|---|---|---|---|---|---|---|---|---|
| | | | | | | | | |
| | | | | | | | | |
| | | | | | | | | |
| | | | | | | | | |
| | | | | | | | | |
| | | | | | | | | |
| | | | | | | | | |
| | | | | | | | | |
| | | | | | | | | |
| | | | | | | | | |

Phase V
Control & Verification

| Date | Party Benefiting | Adjustment Type | Description | Amount Impact | Cumulative Impact | Trigger | Approved By | Status |
|---|---|---|---|---|---|---|---|---|
| | | | | | | | | |
| | | | | | | | | |
| | | | | | | | | |
| | | | | | | | | |
| | | | | | | | | |

**Column Definitions**

**Date**

→ Calendar date

**Party Benefiting**

→ Senior Lender / Junior Lender / Buyer / Seller

**Adjustment Type**

→ Price Reduction / Cash Contribution Increase / Repair Credit / Timeline Extension / Fee Waiver / Condition Modification

**Description**

→ Brief factual summary

**Amount Impact**

→ Dollar amount change (increase or decrease)

**Cumulative Impact**

→ Running total of economic drift

**Trigger**

→ BPO / Junior Demand / Timeline Pressure / Committee Condition

**Approved By**

→ Operator / Committee / Buyer

**Status**

→ Active / Reversed / Superseded

**CUMULATIVE IMPACT SUMMARY**

Total Price Adjustments:

___

Total Buyer Concessions:

___

Total Seller Concessions:

___

Total Lender Concessions:

___

Net Drift From Original Structure:

---

**ECONOMIC CONTROL CHECK**

Has Deal Drifted Outside Target IRR / Return Model?

- □ Yes
- □ No

Has Net-to-Lender Improved or Deteriorated?

- □ Improved
- □ Deteriorated
- □ Neutral

Is Economic Profile Still Acceptable?

- □ Yes
- □ No

Should Kill Criteria Be Revisited?

- □ Yes
- □ No

**STRATEGIC OBSERVATION**

Is Concession Pattern One-Sided?

- □ Yes
- □ No

Is Leverage Increasing or Decreasing?

- □ Increasing
- □ Decreasing
- □ Stable

Primary Economic Risk Remaining:

______________________________________________

Operator Notes:

______________________________________________

______________________________________________

______________________________________________

# Concession & Adjustment Record

Record all material economic concessions and structural adjustments.
Track cumulative impact on net position and risk exposure.

**BASELINE ECONOMIC MODEL**

Original Offer Price:

Original Net-to-Lender Estimate:

Original Buyer Cash Requirement:

Original Seller Contribution:

Original Closing Timeline:

**CONCESSION & ADJUSTMENT TABLE**

| Date | Party Benefiting | Adjustment Type | Description | Amount Impact | Cumulative Impact | Trigger | Approved By | Status |
|---|---|---|---|---|---|---|---|---|
| | | | | | | | | |
| | | | | | | | | |
| | | | | | | | | |
| | | | | | | | | |
| | | | | | | | | |
| | | | | | | | | |
| | | | | | | | | |
| | | | | | | | | |
| | | | | | | | | |
| | | | | | | | | |

| Date | Party Benefiting | Adjustment Type | Description | Amount Impact | Cumulative Impact | Trigger | Approved By | Status |
|---|---|---|---|---|---|---|---|---|
| | | | | | | | | |
| | | | | | | | | |
| | | | | | | | | |
| | | | | | | | | |
| | | | | | | | | |

**Column Definitions**

**Date**

→ Calendar date

**Party Benefiting**

→ Senior Lender / Junior Lender / Buyer / Seller

**Adjustment Type**

→ Price Reduction / Cash Contribution Increase / Repair Credit / Timeline Extension / Fee Waiver / Condition Modification

**Description**

→ Brief factual summary

**Amount Impact**

→ Dollar amount change (increase or decrease)

**Cumulative Impact**

→ Running total of economic drift

**Trigger**

→ BPO / Junior Demand / Timeline Pressure / Committee Condition

**Approved By**

→ Operator / Committee / Buyer

**Status**

→ Active / Reversed / Superseded

**CUMULATIVE IMPACT SUMMARY**

Total Price Adjustments:

_______________________________________________

Total Buyer Concessions:

_______________________________________________

Total Seller Concessions:

_______________________________________________

Total Lender Concessions:

_______________________________________________

Net Drift From Original Structure:

_______________________________________________

## ECONOMIC CONTROL CHECK

Has Deal Drifted Outside Target IRR / Return Model?

- □ Yes
- □ No

Has Net-to-Lender Improved or Deteriorated?

- □ Improved
- □ Deteriorated
- □ Neutral

Is Economic Profile Still Acceptable?

- □ Yes
- □ No

Should Kill Criteria Be Revisited?

- □ Yes
- □ No

## STRATEGIC OBSERVATION

Is Concession Pattern One-Sided?

- □ Yes
- □ No

Is Leverage Increasing or Decreasing?

- □ Increasing
- □ Decreasing
- □ Stable

Primary Economic Risk Remaining:

_______________________________________________

Operator Notes:

_______________________________________________

_______________________________________________

_______________________________________________

# Concession & Adjustment Record

Record all material economic concessions and structural adjustments.
Track cumulative impact on net position and risk exposure.

**BASELINE ECONOMIC MODEL**

Original Offer Price:

Original Net-to-Lender Estimate:

Original Buyer Cash Requirement:

Original Seller Contribution:

Original Closing Timeline:

**CONCESSION & ADJUSTMENT TABLE**

| Date | Party Benefiting | Adjustment Type | Description | Amount Impact | Cumulative Impact | Trigger | Approved By | Status |
|---|---|---|---|---|---|---|---|---|
| | | | | | | | | |
| | | | | | | | | |
| | | | | | | | | |
| | | | | | | | | |
| | | | | | | | | |
| | | | | | | | | |
| | | | | | | | | |
| | | | | | | | | |
| | | | | | | | | |
| | | | | | | | | |

Phase V
Control & Verification

| Date | Party Benefiting | Adjustment Type | Description | Amount Impact | Cumulative Impact | Trigger | Approved By | Status |
|---|---|---|---|---|---|---|---|---|
| | | | | | | | | |
| | | | | | | | | |
| | | | | | | | | |
| | | | | | | | | |
| | | | | | | | | |

**Column Definitions**

**Date**

→ Calendar date

**Party Benefiting**

→ Senior Lender / Junior Lender / Buyer / Seller

**Adjustment Type**

→ Price Reduction / Cash Contribution Increase / Repair Credit / Timeline Extension / Fee Waiver / Condition Modification

**Description**

→ Brief factual summary

**Amount Impact**

→ Dollar amount change (increase or decrease)

**Cumulative Impact**

→ Running total of economic drift

**Trigger**

→ BPO / Junior Demand / Timeline Pressure / Committee Condition

**Approved By**

→ Operator / Committee / Buyer

**Status**

→ Active / Reversed / Superseded

**CUMULATIVE IMPACT SUMMARY**

Total Price Adjustments:

___

Total Buyer Concessions:

___

Total Seller Concessions:

___

Total Lender Concessions:

___

Net Drift From Original Structure:

---

## ECONOMIC CONTROL CHECK

Has Deal Drifted Outside Target IRR / Return Model?

- □ Yes
- □ No

Has Net-to-Lender Improved or Deteriorated?

- □ Improved
- □ Deteriorated
- □ Neutral

Is Economic Profile Still Acceptable?

- □ Yes
- □ No

Should Kill Criteria Be Revisited?

- □ Yes
- □ No

## STRATEGIC OBSERVATION

Is Concession Pattern One-Sided?

- □ Yes
- □ No

Is Leverage Increasing or Decreasing?

- □ Increasing
- □ Decreasing
- □ Stable

Primary Economic Risk Remaining:

________________________________________

Operator Notes:

________________________________________

________________________________________

________________________________________

# Concession & Adjustment Record

Record all material economic concessions and structural adjustments.
Track cumulative impact on net position and risk exposure.

**BASELINE ECONOMIC MODEL**

Original Offer Price:

___

Original Net-to-Lender Estimate:

___

Original Buyer Cash Requirement:

___

Original Seller Contribution:

___

Original Closing Timeline:

___

**CONCESSION & ADJUSTMENT TABLE**

| Date | Party Benefiting | Adjustment Type | Description | Amount Impact | Cumulative Impact | Trigger | Approved By | Status |
|---|---|---|---|---|---|---|---|---|
| | | | | | | | | |
| | | | | | | | | |
| | | | | | | | | |
| | | | | | | | | |
| | | | | | | | | |
| | | | | | | | | |
| | | | | | | | | |
| | | | | | | | | |
| | | | | | | | | |
| | | | | | | | | |

| Date | Party Benefiting | Adjustment Type | Description | Amount Impact | Cumulative Impact | Trigger | Approved By | Status |
|---|---|---|---|---|---|---|---|---|
| | | | | | | | | |
| | | | | | | | | |
| | | | | | | | | |
| | | | | | | | | |
| | | | | | | | | |

**Column Definitions**

**Date**

→ Calendar date

**Party Benefiting**

→ Senior Lender / Junior Lender / Buyer / Seller

**Adjustment Type**

→ Price Reduction / Cash Contribution Increase / Repair Credit / Timeline Extension / Fee Waiver / Condition Modification

**Description**

→ Brief factual summary

**Amount Impact**

→ Dollar amount change (increase or decrease)

**Cumulative Impact**

→ Running total of economic drift

**Trigger**

→ BPO / Junior Demand / Timeline Pressure / Committee Condition

**Approved By**

→ Operator / Committee / Buyer

**Status**

→ Active / Reversed / Superseded

**CUMULATIVE IMPACT SUMMARY**

Total Price Adjustments:

______________________________

Total Buyer Concessions:

______________________________

Total Seller Concessions:

______________________________

Total Lender Concessions:

______________________________

Net Drift From Original Structure:

______________________________

## ECONOMIC CONTROL CHECK

Has Deal Drifted Outside Target IRR / Return Model?

- □ Yes
- □ No

Has Net-to-Lender Improved or Deteriorated?

- □ Improved
- □ Deteriorated
- □ Neutral

Is Economic Profile Still Acceptable?

- □ Yes
- □ No

Should Kill Criteria Be Revisited?

- □ Yes
- □ No

## STRATEGIC OBSERVATION

Is Concession Pattern One-Sided?

- □ Yes
- □ No

Is Leverage Increasing or Decreasing?

- □ Increasing
- □ Decreasing
- □ Stable

Primary Economic Risk Remaining:

_______________________________________________

Operator Notes:

_______________________________________________

_______________________________________________

_______________________________________________

# Final Net Sheet Verification

Verify final settlement statement against approved short sale terms.
Confirm net-to-lender compliance and economic integrity prior to closing.

**APPROVAL REFERENCE**

Short Sale Approval Date:

______________________________

Approval Expiration Date:

______________________________

Approved Net-to-Lender Amount:

______________________________

Approved Sale Price:

______________________________

Approved Junior Settlement Cap (If Applicable):

______________________________

Contribution Requirements (Buyer / Seller):

______________________________

**FINAL SETTLEMENT SUMMARY**

Final Sale Price (HUD / Settlement Statement):

______________________________

Total Closing Costs:

______________________________

Total Junior Payout:

______________________________

Seller Contribution (If Any):

______________________________

Buyer Additional Contributions:

______________________________

Final Net-to-Senior Lender:

______________________________

**VARIANCE ANALYSIS**

Difference Between Approved and Final Net:

______________________________

Variance %:

______________________________

Is Net Below Approval Threshold?

- □ Yes
- □ No

Are All Fees Within Approval Allowances?

- □ Yes
- □ No

Phase V
Control & VerificationHas Any Unapproved Credit Been Added?

Has Any Unapproved Credit Been Added?

□ Yes

□ No

Details of Variance:

______________________________________________________________________

______________________________________________________________________

**PRORATION & ADJUSTMENT REVIEW**

Taxes Prorated Correctly?

□ Yes

□ No

HOA Dues Handled Per Approval?

□ Yes

□ No

Repair Credits Consistent With Approval?

□ Yes

□ No

Title & Recording Fees Accurate?

□ Yes

□ No

Unusual Charges Identified?

□ Yes

□ No

**JUNIOR LIEN CONFIRMATION**

Junior Payout Within Approved Cap?

□ Yes

□ No

Lien Release Confirmed in Writing?

□ Yes

□ No

Deficiency Waiver Confirmed?

□ Yes

□ No

**CONDITION COMPLIANCE CHECK**

Are All Approval Letter Conditions Satisfied?

□ Yes

□ No

Are All Required Affidavits Prepared?

□ Yes

□ No

Is Arm's Length Certification Included?

□ Yes

□ No

Is Occupancy Delivery Condition Satisfied?

- □ Yes
- □ No

## FINAL CONTROL CONFIRMATION

Is Settlement Statement Fully Compliant With Approval?

- □ Yes
- □ No

Is Closing Authorized to Proceed?

- □ Yes
- □ No

Reviewed By:

_______________________________________________

Date:

_______________________________________________

# Pre-Closing Risk Verification

Confirm all material economic, legal, behavioral, and timing risks have been addressed prior to closing authorization.
Document any unresolved exposure before proceeding.

**ECONOMIC RISK CONFIRMATION**

- □ Final Net Sheet Verified Against Approval
- □ No Unauthorized Concessions Added
- □ All Contribution Requirements Satisfied
- □ Junior Settlements Within Approved Limits
- □ Net-to-Lender Meets or Exceeds Approved Threshold

Unresolved Economic Risk Identified?

- □ Yes
- □ No

If Yes, Describe:

---

---

**LEGAL & DOCUMENTATION RISK**

- □ Title Commitment Cleared
- □ All Liens Confirmed Released
- □ Required Affidavits Prepared
- □ Arm's Length Certification Confirmed
- □ Bankruptcy Risk Re-Checked
- □ No Pending Litigation Affecting Closing

Unresolved Legal Risk Identified?

- □ Yes
- □ No

If Yes, Describe:

---

---

**OCCUPANCY & POSSESSION RISK**

- □ Property Condition Verified
- □ Vacant Possession Confirmed (If Required)
- □ Relocation Plan Executed
- □ No Holdover Risk Present
- □ Keys / Access Transfer Plan Confirmed

Unresolved Possession Risk Identified?

- □ Yes
- □ No

If Yes, Describe:

---

**TIMELINE & APPROVAL RISK**

□ Approval Letter Still Valid
□ No Expired Conditions
□ Closing Date Within Approval Window
□ Foreclosure Sale Stayed / Resolved
□ Funding Source Confirmed

Unresolved Timing Risk Identified?

□ Yes
□ No

If Yes, Describe:

---

**BEHAVIORAL & WITHDRAWAL RISK**

□ Seller Commitment Reconfirmed
□ No Bankruptcy Filing Imminent
□ Buyer Performance Verified
□ No Late-Stage Withdrawal Signals

Behavioral Risk Elevated?

□ Yes
□ No

If Yes, Describe:

---

**FINAL RISK CLASSIFICATION**

Overall Pre-Closing Risk Level:

□ Low — Proceed
□ Moderate — Monitor
□ Elevated — Conditional Proceed
□ High — Do Not Close

Is Closing Authorized?

□ Yes
□ No

Authorized By:

---

Date:

---

Signature:

---

# Funding & Closing Checklist

Confirm all funding, documentation, and closing logistics are complete prior to disbursement. Document verification before authorizing wire release and final recording.

**FUNDING CONFIRMATION**

- □ Buyer Funds Verified in Escrow
- □ Wire Instructions Confirmed Directly with Title
- □ Lender Payoff Statement Finalized
- □ Junior Payoff Amount Confirmed
- □ Seller Contribution (If Required) Received
- □ Closing Costs Confirmed Per Settlement Statement

Funding Source:

- □ Cash
- □ Institutional Financing
- □ Private Capital
- □ Other

Wire Release Authorized By:

---

Date:

---

**DOCUMENT EXECUTION**

- □ Deed Executed
- □ Lien Releases Prepared
- □ Affidavits Signed
- □ Arm's Length Certification Executed
- □ Settlement Statement Signed
- □ Closing Disclosure (If Applicable) Reviewed
- □ All Addenda Incorporated

Missing or Outstanding Documents:

---

**TITLE & RECORDING CONTROL**

- □ Title Commitment Cleared
- □ Final Title Policy Ordered
- □ All Liens Confirmed for Release
- □ Recording Package Complete
- □ Recording Fees Verified

Recording Confirmation Number:

---

Date Recorded:

---

## DISBURSEMENT CONTROL

- □ Senior Lender Payoff Wire Confirmed
- □ Junior Lien Payoff Wire Confirmed
- □ Realtor Commissions Disbursed
- □ Relocation Assistance Disbursed (If Applicable)
- □ All Escrow Adjustments Verified

Disbursement Confirmed By:

_______________________________________________

Date:

_______________________________________________

## POST-FUNDING VERIFICATION

- □ Wire Confirmations Retained
- □ Settlement Statement Final Copy Archived
- □ Approval Letter Archived
- □ Lien Release Copies Requested
- □ Updated Title Search Scheduled (If Needed)

File Complete?

- □ Yes
- □ No

## CLOSING AUTHORIZATION CONFIRMATION

Were All Pre-Closing Risk Items Cleared?

- □ Yes
- □ No

Did Closing Occur Within Approval Window?

- □ Yes
- □ No

Were Any Last-Minute Adjustments Made?

- □ Yes
- □ No

If Yes, Logged in Concession Record?

- □ Yes
- □ No

Closing Authorized By:

_______________________________________________

Date:

_______________________________________________

# Title & Lien Clearance Confirmation

Verify all liens, encumbrances, and title defects have been cleared and properly recorded.
Confirm post-closing title integrity and release documentation.

## TITLE POLICY VERIFICATION

Final Title Policy Issued?

- □ Yes
- □ No

Policy Type:

- □ Owner's
- □ Lender's
- □ Both

Policy Number:

___

Effective Date of Policy:

___

Are Exceptions Consistent With Expectations?

- □ Yes
- □ No

Unexpected Exceptions Identified?

- □ Yes
- □ No

If Yes, Describe:

___

___

## SENIOR LIEN RELEASE

Senior Payoff Wire Confirmed?

- □ Yes
- □ No

Lien Release Prepared?

- □ Yes
- □ No

Lien Release Recorded?

- □ Yes
- □ No

Recording Date:

___

Recording Instrument Number:

___

Has Satisfaction Been Verified in County Records?

- □ Yes
- □ No

## JUNIOR LIEN RELEASES

All Junior Payoffs Disbursed?

- □ Yes
- □ No

Lien Release Letters Obtained?

- □ Yes
- □ No

Lien Releases Recorded?

- □ Yes
- □ No

Recording Instrument Numbers:

___

Is Any Lien Release Pending?

- □ Yes
- □ No

If Yes, Describe:

___

## ADDITIONAL ENCUMBRANCES

Judgments Cleared?

- □ Yes
- □ No

Tax Liens Cleared?

- □ Yes
- □ No

HOA Liens Cleared?

- □ Yes
- □ No

Mechanics Liens Cleared?

- □ Yes
- □ No

UCC Filings Addressed?

- □ Yes
- □ No

Outstanding Encumbrance Identified?

- □ Yes
- □ No

## POST-CLOSING TITLE REVIEW

Post-Recording Title Search Completed?

- □ Yes
- □ No

Are All Liens Showing as Released?

- □ Yes
- □ No

Phase V
Control & VerificationIs Title Marketable?

Is Title Marketable?

□ Yes

□ No

Any Residual Exposure Identified?

□ Yes

□ No

## DEFICIENCY WAIVER CONFIRMATION

Deficiency Waiver Confirmed in Writing?

□ Yes

□ No

Release Language Archived?

□ Yes

□ No

Does Release Fully Cover Seller?

□ Yes

□ No

## FINAL TITLE CLEARANCE CERTIFICATION

All Liens Cleared and Recorded?

□ Yes

□ No

All Releases Verified?

□ Yes

□ No

File Fully Archived?

□ Yes

□ No

Title Clearance Confirmed By:

_______________________________________________

Date:

_______________________________________________

Signature:

_______________________________________________

# Post-Closing Capital Deployment Plan

Define post-closing capital allocation, stabilization sequencing, and risk containment measures. Document disciplined deployment aligned with original investment thesis.

**INITIAL CAPITAL POSITION**

Total Capital Raised:

---

Acquisition Cost (All-In):

---

Closing Costs:

---

Remaining Operating Liquidity:

---

Debt Structure Post-Closing:

---

Cash Reserve After Close:

---

Is Liquidity Adequate for 6–12 Months?

□ Yes

□ No

**STABILIZATION PRIORITIES**

Immediate Repair Items (0–30 Days):

---

---

Short-Term Improvements (30–120 Days):

---

---

Long-Term Improvements (120+ Days):

---

Is Capital Deployment Sequenced?

□ Yes

□ No

**CAPEX DEPLOYMENT TABLE**

| Project | Budgeted Amount | Actual Spend | Funding Source | Timeline | Expected Impact | Status |
|---|---|---|---|---|---|---|
| | | | | | | |
| | | | | | | |
| | | | | | | |

Phase V
Control & Verification

| Project | Budgeted Amount | Actual Spend | Funding Source | Timeline | Expected Impact | Status |
|---|---|---|---|---|---|---|
| | | | | | | |
| | | | | | | |
| | | | | | | |
| | | | | | | |
| | | | | | | |
| | | | | | | |
| | | | | | | |

**REVENUE STABILIZATION STRATEGY**

Occupancy Target:

______________________________________________

Rent Adjustment Plan:

______________________________________________

Lease-Up Strategy:

______________________________________________

Marketing Channel Focus:

______________________________________________

Time to Stabilization Target (Months):

______________________________________________

**RISK CONTAINMENT MEASURES**

Insurance Coverage Updated?

□ Yes
□ No

Property Management Engaged?

□ Yes
□ No

Vendor Controls Established?

□ Yes
□ No

Operating Budget Approved?

□ Yes
□ No

Unexpected Post-Closing Risk Identified?

- □ Yes
- □ No

**EXIT STRATEGY ALIGNMENT**

Target Hold Period:

---

Exit Strategy:

- □ Refinance
- □ Sale
- □ Portfolio Aggregation
- □ Long-Term Hold

Target Cap Rate at Exit:

---

Target IRR / Return Objective:

---

Is Original Investment Thesis Intact?

- □ Yes
- □ No

If No, Why:

---

**CAPITAL DISCIPLINE REVIEW**

Is Deployment Within Original Budget?

- □ Yes
- □ No

Has Capital Drift Occurred?

- □ Yes
- □ No

Is Additional Capital Required?

- □ Yes
- □ No

Should Return Projections Be Updated?

- □ Yes
- □ No

Operator Notes:

---

---

# Verification V – Control

## PRE-CLOSING ADVANCEMENT AUTHORIZATION

### CAPITAL AUTHORIZATION REQUIRED

Closing is authorized only when all economic, legal, title, funding, and behavioral risks have been reviewed and confirmed within acceptable thresholds.
Capital deployment and liability assumption occur upon execution of closing documents.

### ECONOMIC & NET POSITION VERIFICATION

□ Final Net Sheet Verified Against Approval
□ Net-to-Lender Meets or Exceeds Approved Threshold
□ All Concessions Within Approval Terms
□ Junior Lien Settlements Confirmed
□ No Unauthorized Credits
□ Capital Contribution Amount Confirmed

### LEGAL & TITLE CONFIRMATION

□ Title Commitment Cleared
□ All Liens Identified and Addressed
□ Lien Releases Prepared
□ Deficiency Waiver Confirmed (if applicable)
□ Required Affidavits Executed

Residual Legal Exposure Present?

□ Yes
□ No

If Yes, Document:

→ Writing Line
→ Writing Line

### TIMING & FUNDING CONTROL

□ Approval Letter Valid
□ Closing Within Approved Window
□ Buyer Funds Verified
□ Wire Instructions Confirmed
□ Disbursement Instructions Reviewed

Timing Risk Acceptable?

□ Yes
□ No

### DEFICIENCIES / CONDITIONS

If authorization is conditional, document mitigation plan.

→ Writing Line
→ Writing Line

## ADVANCEMENT STATUS

- □ Authorized — Proceed to Closing
- □ Authorized with Conditions
- □ Defer Closing
- □ Do Not Close

## AUTHORIZATION

### Execution Authority (Transaction Lead)

Name: ______________________________

Title / Role: _________________________

Signature: ___________________________

Date: _______________________________

### Capital Authority (Managing Member / GP / Investor Representative)

Name: ______________________________

Title / Role: _________________________

Signature: ___________________________

Date: _______________________________

Authority Basis (if applicable):

- □ Sole Operator
- □ Managing Member
- □ General Partner
- □ Investment Committee
- □ Other

## Phase V — Structured Notes

Document observations, tactical considerations, or material developments not captured in structured worksheets.
Maintain objective, execution-focused notation.

# PHASE VI
# POST-MORTEM & REFINEMENT

# Orientation

**Phase VI evaluates performance and system integrity.**

This phase analyzes:

- Profit and variance
- Timeline efficiency
- Risk events
- Structural weaknesses
- Repeatability

The objective is refinement.

This phase strengthens future execution.

No advancement follows.

Only improvement.

***"Reflection Strengthens Judgment."***

# Profit & Variance Analysis

Compare projected financial performance to actual results.
Identify material variances and document contributing factors objectively.

## ORIGINAL UNDERWRITING SUMMARY

Projected Purchase Price:

Projected All-In Cost:

Projected Net-to-Lender:

Projected Stabilized Value:

Projected Exit Cap Rate:

Projected IRR / ROI:

Projected Hold Period:

## ACTUAL PERFORMANCE SUMMARY

Actual Purchase Price:

Actual All-In Cost:

Actual Stabilized Value (If Sold):

Actual Exit Cap Rate (If Sold):

Actual IRR / ROI:

Actual Hold Period:

Current Valuation (If Holding):

## VARIANCE TABLE

| Metric | Projected | Actual | Variance ($/%) | Favorable / Unfavorable | Primary Cause |
|---|---|---|---|---|---|
| Purchase Price | | | | | |
| All-In Cost | | | | | |
| Repair Budget | | | | | |
| Time to Stabilization | | | | | |
| Exit Price / Valuation | | | | | |
| IRR / Return | | | | | |

## COST OVERRUN ANALYSIS

Were Repairs Within Budget?

□ Yes

□ No

Were Closing Costs Accurate?

□ Yes

□ No

Did Carrying Costs Exceed Model?

□ Yes

□ No

Primary Cause of Cost Variance:

______________________________________________________________________

______________________________________________________________________

## REVENUE PERFORMANCE REVIEW

Was Lease-Up Timeline Accurate?

□ Yes

□ No

Were Rent Projections Realistic?

□ Yes

□ No

Did Market Conditions Shift?

□ Yes

□ No

Did Vacancy Exceed Projections?

□ Yes

□ No

Primary Cause of Revenue Variance:

______________________________________________________________________

______________________________________________________________________

## TIMELINE VARIANCE

Was Negotiation Timeline Accurate?

□ Yes

□ No

Did Approval Delays Impact Carry?

□ Yes

□ No

Did Execution Delays Affect Returns?

□ Yes

□ No

Months of Variance From Plan:

______________________________________________________________________

**RISK MODEL ACCURACY**

Were Identified Risks Accurate?

- □ Yes
- □ No

Did Unexpected Risks Occur?

- □ Yes
- □ No

Were Behavioral Risk Assessments Accurate?

- □ Yes
- □ No

Were Kill Criteria Correctly Calibrated?

- □ Yes
- □ No

**LESSONS & MODEL ADJUSTMENTS**

What Assumptions Were Incorrect?

______________________________________________

What Controls Worked?

______________________________________________

What Would Be Underwritten Differently Next Time?

______________________________________________

______________________________________________

Should Return Hurdles Be Adjusted?

- □ Yes
- □ No

**OVERALL PERFORMANCE CLASSIFICATION**

Deal Performance Relative to Model:

- □ Outperformed
- □ Met Expectations
- □ Underperformed

Would This Deal Be Repeated Under Similar Conditions?

- □ Yes
- □ No

Operator Signature:

______________________________________________

Date:

______________________________________________

# Timeline Performance Review

Compare projected transaction timeline to actual performance.
Identify delays, bottlenecks, and structural breakdowns objectively.

## ORIGINAL TIMELINE MODEL

Projected Intake to Submission (Days):

---

Projected Submission to Approval (Days):

---

Projected Approval to Closing (Days):

---

Projected Total Transaction Duration (Days):

---

Projected Stabilization Period (Months):

---

## ACTUAL TIMELINE PERFORMANCE

Actual Intake to Submission (Days):

---

Actual Submission to Approval (Days):

---

Actual Approval to Closing (Days):

---

Actual Total Transaction Duration (Days):

---

Actual Stabilization Period (Months):

---

## TIMELINE VARIANCE TABLE

| Phase Segment | Projected Duration | Actual Duration | Variance (Days) | Favorable / Unfavorable | Primary Cause |
|---|---|---|---|---|---|
| Intake → Structuring | | | | | |
| Submission → Valuation | | | | | |
| Valuation → Approval | | | | | |
| Approval → Closing | | | | | |
| Stabilization → Exit | | | | | |

## DELAY SOURCE ANALYSIS

Primary Delay Driver:

- □ Seller
- □ Senior Lender
- □ Junior Lienholder
- □ Buyer
- □ Title / Legal
- □ Market Conditions

□ Operator

Phase VI
Post-Mortem & RefinementSecondary Delay Driver:

Secondary Delay Driver:

______________________________________________________________________

Was Delay Predictable?

- □ Yes
- □ No

Was Delay Preventable?

- □ Yes
- □ No

**FORECLOSURE & CLOCK PRESSURE REVIEW**

Did Foreclosure Timeline Impact Negotiation?

- □ Yes
- □ No

Were Extensions Required?

- □ Yes
- □ No

Did Expiration Risk Affect Leverage?

- □ Yes
- □ No

Did Approval Expiration Require Rework?

- □ Yes
- □ No

**PROCESS BOTTLENECK IDENTIFICATION**

Where Did File Stall Most?

______________________________________________________________________

Was Escalation Used Appropriately?

- □ Yes
- □ No

Did Communication Gaps Contribute to Delay?

- □ Yes
- □ No

Was Internal Task Control Adequate?

- □ Yes
- □ No

**TIMELINE IMPACT ON RETURNS**

Did Carry Costs Exceed Model Due to Delay?

- □ Yes
- □ No

Did IRR Decrease Due to Timeline Drift?

- □ Yes
- □ No

Estimated IRR Impact of Delay:

______________________________________________________________________

Was Additional Capital Required Due to Delay?

□ Yes

□ No

**STRUCTURAL REFINEMENT NOTES**

Which Phase Requires Tighter Control?

___

What Structural Change Would Reduce Delay?

___

Should Timeline Assumptions Be Adjusted in Future Models?

□ Yes

□ No

Revised Baseline Timeline (Future Deals):

**OVERALL TIMELINE CLASSIFICATION**

Timeline Performance:

□ Ahead of Model

□ On Target

□ Delayed

□ Severely Delayed

Was Delay Economically Material?

□ Yes

□ No

Would Timeline Risk Change Future Kill Criteria?

□ Yes

□ No

Operator Signature:

___

Date:

___

# Risk Events & Resolution Log

Document material risk events that occurred during the transaction.
Record impact, response actions, and final resolution objectively.

**RISK EVENT LOG TABLE**

| Event ID | Date Identified | Risk Category | Description of Event | Impact Severity | Action Taken | Resolution Strategy | Time to Resolution (Days) | Final Outcome | Preventable? |
|---|---|---|---|---|---|---|---|---|---|
| | | | | | | | | | |
| | | | | | | | | | |
| | | | | | | | | | |
| | | | | | | | | | |
| | | | | | | | | | |
| | | | | | | | | | |
| | | | | | | | | | |
| | | | | | | | | | |
| | | | | | | | | | |
| | | | | | | | | | |
| | | | | | | | | | |
| | | | | | | | | | |
| | | | | | | | | | |
| | | | | | | | | | |

| Event ID | Date Identified | Risk Category | Description of Event | Impact Severity | Action Taken | Resolution Strategy | Time to Resolution (Days) | Final Outcome | Preventable? |
|---|---|---|---|---|---|---|---|---|---|
| | | | | | | | | | |

**Risk Category** (Suggested Values)

- Seller Behavioral
- Bankruptcy Threat
- Junior Lien Holdout
- BPO Dispute
- Title Defect
- Foreclosure Acceleration
- Funding Delay
- Buyer Performance
- Legal / Litigation
- Market Shift
- Operational / Execution
- Other

**Impact Severity**

- Low
- Moderate
- High
- Critical

## RISK PATTERN ANALYSIS

Number of Risk Events Logged:

---

Most Frequent Risk Category:

---

Longest Resolution Duration (Days):

---

Did Any Risk Nearly Terminate the Deal?

□ Yes

□ No

If Yes, Which Event ID:

---

## RESPONSE EFFECTIVENESS REVIEW

Were Risk Controls Adequate?

□ Yes

□ No

Was Escalation Used Appropriately?

□ Yes

□ No

Was Mitigation Reactive or Proactive?

□ Reactive

□ Proactive

Were Kill Criteria Revisited During Risk Event?

□ Yes

□ No

## PREVENTABILITY ASSESSMENT

Could This Risk Have Been Identified Earlier?

□ Yes

□ No

Would Stronger Gate Discipline Have Reduced Exposure?

□ Yes

□ No

Does Underwriting Model Need Adjustment?

□ Yes

□ No

Structural Change Required in Future Deals?

□ Yes

□ No

## LESSON CAPTURE

Most Expensive Risk Event:

---

Most Disruptive Risk Event:

What Early Signal Was Missed (If Any):

System Improvement Required:

# What Worked / What Failed

Identify strategies, controls, and decisions that contributed positively or negatively to transaction performance.
Document objectively without narrative justification.

**WHAT WORKED**

Strategic Decisions That Strengthened Position:

Negotiation Tactics That Increased Leverage:

Risk Controls That Prevented Loss:

Gate Discipline That Preserved Net Position:

Timeline Controls That Reduced Drift:

Behavioral Assessments That Proved Accurate:

Unexpected Advantages Realized:

**WHAT FAILED**

Underwriting Assumptions That Were Incorrect:

Negotiation Approaches That Reduced Leverage:

Risk Signals Missed:

Process Breakdowns:

Timeline Miscalculations:

Capital Deployment Errors:

Communication Failures:

Escalation Delays or Missteps:

## STRUCTURAL WEAKNESS IDENTIFICATION

Which Phase Was Weakest?

- □ Phase I — Intake
- □ Phase II — Feasibility
- □ Phase III — Structuring
- □ Phase IV — Execution
- □ Phase V — Control
- □ Phase VI — Post-Mortem

Was Weakness Structural or Situational?

- □ Structural
- □ Situational

If Structural, Describe Required Change:

---

## LEVERAGE & POSITION REVIEW

Did You Lose Leverage at Any Point?

- □ Yes
- □ No

If Yes, Why:

---

Was Kill Criteria Ever Ignored?

- □ Yes
- □ No

Did Emotional Bias Influence a Decision?

- □ Yes
- □ No

## REPEATABILITY ASSESSMENT

Would This Strategy Be Used Again?

- □ Yes
- □ No

Would This Counterparty Be Engaged Again?

- □ Yes
- □ No

Would This Lender Process Be Pursued Again?

- □ Yes
- □ No

Was Risk-Reward Appropriate?

- □ Yes
- □ No

## OPERATOR CERTIFICATION

This review was conducted without narrative rationalization and reflects objective assessment.
Operator Signature:

---

Phase VI
Post-Mortem & RefinementDate:

Date:

# Process Refinement Notes (Multiple Pages)

Document structural improvements to the Short Sale Control System identified during this transaction. Record refinements that will strengthen future execution discipline.

## PHASE-BASED REFINEMENT REVIEW

### Phase I — Intake

Were initial risk flags sufficient?

□ Yes

□ No

Should additional intake metrics be added?

□ Yes

□ No

Recommended Intake Refinement:

________________________________________

________________________________________

### Phase II — Feasibility

Was valuation modeling accurate?

□ Yes

□ No

Should feasibility stress thresholds be adjusted?

□ Yes

□ No

Recommended Feasibility Refinement:

________________________________________

________________________________________

### Phase III — Structuring

Was offer structuring optimal?

□ Yes

□ No

Did leverage deteriorate due to structure?

□ Yes

□ No

Recommended Structuring Refinement:

________________________________________

________________________________________

### Phase IV — Execution

Was submission discipline adequate?

□ Yes

□ No

Was escalation timing effective?

□ Yes

□ No

Recommended Execution Refinement:

________________________________________

________________________________________

**Phase V — Control & Verification**

Were gates triggered appropriately?

□ Yes

□ No

Should additional verification checkpoints exist?

□ Yes

□ No

Recommended Control Refinement:

______________________________________________

______________________________________________

**Phase VI — Post-Mortem**

Was analysis sufficiently rigorous?

□ Yes

□ No

Should new tracking metrics be added?

□ Yes

□ No

Recommended Post-Mortem Refinement:

______________________________________________

______________________________________________

## CONTROL SYSTEM MODIFICATION LOG

| Refinement ID | Phase Affected | Description of Change | Reason for Change | Implementation Date | Applied to Future Deals? |
|---|---|---|---|---|---|
| | | | | | |
| | | | | | |
| | | | | | |
| | | | | | |
| | | | | | |
| | | | | | |
| | | | | | |
| | | | | | |

Phase VI
Post-Mortem & Refinement

| Refinement ID | Phase Affected | Description of Change | Reason for Change | Implementation Date | Applied to Future Deals? |
|---|---|---|---|---|---|
| | | | | | |
| | | | | | |
| | | | | | |
| | | | | | |

**METRIC ADJUSTMENT REVIEW**

Should Risk Scoring Thresholds Be Adjusted?

□ Yes

□ No

Should Kill Criteria Be Raised?

□ Yes

□ No

Should Return Hurdles Be Increased?

□ Yes

□ No

Should Timeline Assumptions Be Extended?

□ Yes

□ No

Describe Structural Threshold Changes:

______________________________________________

______________________________________________

**SYSTEM EVOLUTION NOTES**

What structural lesson most materially improves the system?

______________________________________________

What recurring weakness must be eliminated?

______________________________________________

What capability should be strengthened next?

______________________________________________

Is the Short Sale Control System materially stronger after this deal?

□ Yes

□ No

## Repeatability Checklist

Evaluate whether this transaction structure, counterparty profile, and execution model are suitable for repetition.
Assess scalability without narrative justification.

### DEAL STRUCTURE REPEATABILITY

Was Entry Basis Sufficiently Protected?

- □ Yes
- □ No

Was Net-to-Lender Model Replicable?

- □ Yes
- □ No

Was Risk Properly Priced?

- □ Yes
- □ No

Did Structure Depend on Unusual Concessions?

- □ Yes
- □ No

Did Outcome Depend on Atypical Market Conditions?

- □ Yes
- □ No

Is Similar Opportunity Frequency Predictable?

- □ Yes
- □ No

### COUNTERPARTY REPEATABILITY

Was Seller Cooperation Sufficient?

- □ Yes
- □ No

Was Lender Behavior Predictable?

- □ Yes
- □ No

Were Junior Liens Manageable?

- □ Yes
- □ No

Would You Engage This Lender Again?

- □ Yes
- □ No

Would You Pursue This Counterparty Profile Again?

- □ Yes
- □ No

### PROCESS SCALABILITY

Did the Control System Handle Risk Adequately?

- □ Yes
- □ No

Was Timeline Drift Acceptable?

Phase VI
Post-Mortem & Refinement□ Yes

- □ Yes
- □ No

Was Capital Deployment Controlled?

- □ Yes
- □ No

Could This Deal Be Managed Simultaneously With 3–5 Others?

- □ Yes
- □ No

Did Execution Require Extraordinary Effort?

- □ Yes
- □ No

Was Stress Load Sustainable?

- □ Yes
- □ No

## CAPITAL EFFICIENCY REVIEW

Was Return Adequate for Risk Taken?

- □ Yes
- □ No

Did Capital Remain Locked Longer Than Modeled?

- □ Yes
- □ No

Was Liquidity Pressure Excessive?

- □ Yes
- □ No

Did IRR Justify Complexity?

- □ Yes
- □ No

## SYSTEM DEPENDENCY CHECK

Did Success Depend on:

- Operator Judgment Beyond Model?
  - □ Yes
  - □ No
- Unplanned Relationship Leverage?
  - □ Yes
  - □ No
- External Market Tailwinds?
  - □ Yes
  - □ No
- Unrepeatable Timing Factors?
  - □ Yes
  - □ No

## REPEATABILITY CLASSIFICATION

Overall Deal Classification:

□ Fully Repeatable
□ Repeatable With Refinement
□ Opportunistic Only
□ Do Not Repeat

Would You Pursue This Exact Structure Again?

□ Yes
□ No

Would You Scale This Model?

□ Yes
□ No

Recommended Future Positioning:

---

**STRATEGIC CONCLUSION**

This deal represents:

□ Core Strategy
□ Secondary Strategy
□ Situational Strategy
□ Avoid Category

Operator Signature:

---

Date:

---

## Phase VI — Structured Notes

Document observations, tactical considerations, or material developments not captured in structured worksheets.
Maintain objective, execution-focused notation.

# APPENDIX

# Deal Archive Cover Sheet

Complete upon transaction closure.
Attach to front of archived physical or digital file.

## DEAL IDENTIFICATION

Project Name:

Property Address:

City / State / ZIP:

Property Type:

Deal Classification:

- □ Short Sale — Residential
- □ Short Sale — Commercial
- □ Multi-Lien Short Sale
- □ Distressed Acquisition
- □ Other

File Number / Internal ID:

## TRANSACTION SUMMARY

Contract Execution Date:

Submission Date:

Approval Date:

Closing Date:

Total Transaction Duration (Days):

Final Sale Price:

Final Net-to-Senior Lender:

Total Capital Invested (If Applicable):

## PERFORMANCE CLASSIFICATION

Outcome Classification:

- □ Exceeded Model
- □ Met Model
- □ Underperformed

□ Terminated

Termination Reason (If Applicable):

_______________________________________________

Repeatability Classification:

□ Fully Repeatable

□ Repeatable With Refinement

□ Opportunistic

□ Do Not Repeat

**RISK SUMMARY SNAPSHOT**

Number of Material Risk Events Logged:

_______________________________________________

Highest Risk Category Encountered:

_______________________________________________

Was Foreclosure Threat Active?

□ Yes

□ No

Was Bankruptcy Threat Present?

□ Yes

□ No

Were Junior Liens Present?

□ Yes

□ No

**ARCHIVE STATUS**

All Documents Archived?

□ Yes

□ No

All Releases Recorded?

□ Yes

□ No

Title Policy Confirmed?

□ Yes

□ No

Financial Performance Recorded?

□ Yes

□ No

System Refinements Logged?

□ Yes

□ No

File Status:

□ Closed — Complete

□ Closed — Pending Final Documentation

□ Terminated — Archived

□ Active Monitoring Required

## OPERATOR CERTIFICATION

This file is complete and accurately reflects the transaction record.
Operator Name:

---

Signature:

---

Date:

---

# Investor Reporting Template

Use for structured communication with capital partners.
Provide objective performance updates and forward outlook.

## PROJECT IDENTIFICATION

Project Name:

______________________________

Property Address:

______________________________

Reporting Period:

______________________________

Reporting Date:

______________________________

Operator:

______________________________

## EXECUTIVE SUMMARY

Current Project Status:

______________________________

Major Milestones Achieved This Period:

______________________________

______________________________

Material Issues or Risks:

______________________________

______________________________

Overall Performance Classification:

- □ On Track
- □ Ahead of Plan
- □ Minor Variance
- □ Material Variance

## FINANCIAL SUMMARY

| Metric | Original Projection | Current Projection | Actual to Date | Variance |
|---|---|---|---|---|
| | | | | |
| Acquisition Cost | | | | |
| Total Capital Invested | | | | |
| Capital Remaining | | | | |
| Operating Income (If Stabilized) | | | | |
| Carrying Costs | | | | |
| Net Position | | | | |
| Projected IRR | | | | |
| Projected Exit Value | | | | |

## CAPITAL POSITION

Total Capital Raised:

______________________________

Capital Deployed to Date:

---

Remaining Reserves:

---

Is Additional Capital Required?

- □ Yes
- □ No

If Yes, Explanation:

---

---

**TIMELINE UPDATE**

Original Closing Target:

---

Actual Closing Date:

---

Stabilization Target:

---

Revised Stabilization Target (If Applicable):

---

Is Timeline Drift Material?

- □ Yes
- □ No

**RISK UPDATE**

Material Risk Events This Period:

---

Mitigation Actions Taken:

---

Foreclosure Risk Present?

- □ Yes
- □ No

Bankruptcy Risk Present?

- □ Yes
- □ No

Approval Risk Present?

- □ Yes
- □ No

Overall Risk Level:

- □ Low
- □ Moderate
- □ Elevated

## FORWARD OUTLOOK

Next Major Milestone:

_______________________________________________

Expected Timeline to Next Milestone:

_______________________________________________

Strategic Focus Next Period:

_______________________________________________

Is Exit Strategy Intact?

- □ Yes
- □ No

## DISTRIBUTION STATUS

Distributions Made This Period?

- □ Yes
- □ No

Distribution Amount:

_______________________________________________

Projected Next Distribution (If Applicable):

_______________________________________________

## CERTIFICATION

This report reflects accurate financial and operational status as of the reporting date.

Operator Name:

_______________________________________________

Signature:

_______________________________________________

Date:

_______________________________________________

## Acronyms and Terms

**Approval Letter** — Written lender authorization outlining approved short sale terms, net requirements, and conditions. (Phase IV, Phase V)

**Arm's Length Certification** — Signed statement confirming no undisclosed relationships between buyer and seller. (Phase IV, Phase V)

**Arrearage** — Total past-due loan amount including missed payments, fees, and penalties. (Phase I, Phase II)

**Bankruptcy Risk** — Probability that borrower files protection, potentially halting foreclosure or short sale. (Phase II, Phase IV)

**BPO (Broker Price Opinion)** — Lender-ordered property valuation used to determine acceptable sale price. (Phase IV)

**Capital Stack** — Structure of funding sources including senior debt, junior liens, and equity. (Phase II, Phase III)

**Carrying Costs** — Ongoing expenses incurred while holding property prior to stabilization or exit. (Phase II, Phase VI)

**Concession** — Financial adjustment or credit reducing net-to-lender or increasing buyer benefit. (Phase III, Phase IV, Phase V)

**Counteroffer** — Lender-proposed revision to submitted short sale terms.

**Deficiency Waiver** — Written release from lender absolving borrower of remaining debt after short sale. (Phase V)

**Distress Indicator** — Observable signal of financial or behavioral instability affecting transaction viability. (Phase I, Phase II)

**Escalation** — Formal request to elevate file to higher-level decision authority within lender organization. (Phase IV)

**Execution Risk** — Probability that process breakdown prevents closing after approval. (Phase IV, Phase V)

**Foreclosure Timeline** — Statutory or lender-driven process toward property auction if loan default is unresolved. (Phase I, Phase IV)

**Gate (Verification Gate)** — Structured checkpoint requiring confirmation before advancing phases. (Phase III, Phase V)

**Hardship Narrative** — Borrower explanation supporting inability to satisfy loan obligation. (Phase IV)

**IRR (Internal Rate of Return)** — Annualized return metric used to evaluate capital performance. (Phase II, Phase VI)

**Intake** — Initial data-gathering and file structuring stage of the transaction. (Phase I)

**Junior Lien** — Secondary secured debt subordinate to senior mortgage. (Phase I, Phase III, Phase IV)

**Kill Criteria** — Predefined conditions requiring termination of the deal. (Phase II, Phase VI)

**Lien Priority** — Order in which secured creditors are paid from sale proceeds. (Phase I, Phase II)

**Loss Mitigation** — Lender department responsible for managing defaulted loans and short sales. (Phase IV)

**Market Value Estimation** — Structured valuation based on comparable sales and condition analysis. (Phase II)

**Net-to-Lender** — Final funds received by senior lienholder after approved deductions. (Phase II, Phase V)

**Operator** — Individual or entity executing the Short Sale Control System. (All Phases)

**Pre-Closing Verification** — Final structured risk review prior to settlement authorization. (Phase V)

**Projected Stabilization** — Modeled timeline to achieve target occupancy or income performance. (Phase II, Phase VI)

**Risk Flag** — Identified exposure requiring monitoring or mitigation. (Phase I, Phase II)

**Short Sale** — Transaction in which lender agrees to accept less than full loan payoff to resolve default. (All Phases)

**Stabilization** — Period during which property performance is brought to targeted operational level. (Phase VI)

**Submission Package** — Compiled documentation delivered to lender for short sale review. (Phase IV)

**Timeline Drift** — Deviation between projected and actual transaction duration. (Phase VI)

**Title Commitment** — Preliminary title report identifying liens and encumbrances prior to closing. (Phase V)

**Variance** — Measurable difference between projected and actual financial or timeline outcomes. (Phase VI)

# Global Structured Notes

Document observations, tactical considerations, or material developments not captured in structured worksheets.
Maintain objective, execution-focused notation.

www.ingramcontent.com/pod-product-compliance
Lightning Source LLC
Chambersburg PA
CBHW061352240926
51846CB00007B/1381
*9781972137994*